PENGUIN BOOKS
Remembering Rachel

Rose Duff was born in 1941 and reared in Dublin among a family of nine children. At nineteen she met and fell in love with Jim Callaly, and they married when Rose was twenty-four. Together they adopted five children, with Rose becoming a full-time mother and housewife – enjoying family life in a time when life was simpler and society more secure. Rose and Jim were blessed with ongoing health and happiness and became grandparents for the first time in 2000, when their elder daughter, Rachel, gave birth to her first child.

The unimaginable tragedy of Rachel's murder in October 2004 led Rose to write this account of her daughter's death and its aftermath. Though at times it was an agonizing process, Rose was determined to create this testimony and a tribute to Rachel's memory. Rose and Jim Callaly still live in Dublin, surrounded by the love of their four children, Declan, Paul, Ann and Anthony, their daughters-in-law, Denise and Denise, and their six grandchildren.

Remembering Rachel

A True Story of Betrayal and Murder

ROSE CALLALY

PENGUIN BOOKS

PENGUIN BOOKS

Published by the Penguin Group
Penguin Books Ltd, 80 Strand, London wc2r orl, England
Penguin Group (USA) Inc., 375 Hudson Street, New York, New York 10014, USA
Penguin Group (Canada), 90 Eglinton Avenue East, Suite 700, Toronto, Ontario, Canada m4p 2y3
(a division of Pearson Penguin Canada Inc.)
Penguin Ireland, 25 St Stephen's Green, Dublin 2, Ireland (a division of Penguin Books Ltd)
Penguin Group (Australia), 250 Camberwell Road,
Camberwell, Victoria 3124, Australia (a division of Pearson Australia Group Pty Ltd)
Penguin Books India Pvt Ltd, 11 Community Centre, Panchsheel Park,
New Delhi – 110 017, India
Penguin Group (NZ), 67 Apollo Drive, Rosedale, North Shore 0632, New Zealand
(a division of Pearson New Zealand Ltd)
Penguin Books (South Africa) (Pty) Ltd, 24 Sturdee Avenue, Rosebank, Johannesburg 2196,
South Africa

Penguin Books Ltd, Registered Offices: 80 Strand, London wc2r orl, England

www.penguin.com

First published by Penguin Ireland 2009
Published in Penguin Books 2010
1

To my darling Rachel,

May this book forever reflect your
beautiful spirit.

Remembering Rachel's little ones.

Contents

Author's Note

From the very first moment Joe O'Reilly rang our house that awful day, I knew that something terrible had happened. Nothing on this earth could have prepared me for the horror of the days and months we were to endure as the truth of what had really happened started to emerge. Everything about losing a child is painful; it is something that no parent ever wants to have to face, but when it happens through extreme violence and at the hands of the one person your child loved unconditionally and trusted with her life, it is the worst pain imaginable. The murder of your child changes your life for ever.

After the initial shock and the pain of knowing you can never see your child again, the process goes on and on. You get through the days having to endure the identification of the body, the funeral, the investigation and eventually the trial and possible appeal. Murder is a crime that continues to destroy a family every single day. It is now five years since our daughter Rachel was murdered by her husband, and we now realize that the pain, sadness, anger and loneliness that grips our family will never go away.

One of the hardest things for me about Rachel's murder was the invasion of her privacy as the most intimate parts of her life were laid bare for the world to see. I do not want people to remember Rachel by the awful names she was called, or the way she was portrayed by people who do not know what love is. I want her story, the true story of her life and how she lived it, to be known. I have written this book to tell that story and to try to give an insight into the kind of person Rachel really was. It has been almost impossible at times to get it all down on paper, not only because of the emotions it brought to the surface, but because there aren't enough words to express the true horror of our daughter's brutal murder and the effect it has had on all our family.

In telling Rachel's story, my goal was to be honest and to honour our daughter's memory. I have tried to remember the details of these excruciating five years as honestly as I could. Obviously, it has been a very traumatic and upsetting period in our lives, and between time passing, repeating statements for the Garda and the courts, and the extensive media coverage, the details have at times become hazy. I have done my utmost to describe things as they happened, but my recollection of small matters of detail may not be 100 per cent accurate. If I have made errors, I have not done so intentionally.

In the midst of all this, my priority has been to protect our grandchildren, Rachel's children. This is still my priority and for that reason, although they are a crucial part of Rachel's story, I have gone to considerable lengths to respect and protect their privacy.

Introduction: The True
Story of Rachel's Life

'All rise.' That phrase will always have the power
to bring me right back to when we sat in Court
Number 2. I can still feel what it was like when
Judge Barry White's tipstaff would announce his
arrival, and he would make his way back into the
court, all eyes on him, and the trial would then
continue. Day by day, we were being shown that
our daughter Rachel's life with her husband, Joe,
was far from the ideal picture of a happy family
they gave the appearance of being. It makes you
wonder how well we really know people and what
goes on in the lives we think we know so well.
Learning that my own daughter had a life so
different to what I thought has changed for ever

not only the way I think about what I see, but also what I think I understand.

The marriage that had started out with such excitement for Rachel, the dream life with Joe that was all she ever wanted, turned out to cause her enormous pain and hurt. She could never give him what he thought he needed. Day after day, we were finding out that he had a cruel and irrepressible need to destroy his wife and let him move on. We will never be able to get over the way Joe O'Reilly systematically and intentionally tried to devalue and erode any self-esteem Rachel had left. He never showed any sense of fairness or justice towards Rachel or her memory and he carefully planned to rob Rachel and her children of their future together. Cruelly, that was not enough for him. Joe O'Reilly was so bitter and so resentful of his beautiful and popular young wife, he decided to rid his life of her entirely.

Joe appeared to be fairly normal to us, but he was able to mask his true personality. I can now see quite clearly how manipulative he was, that he really believed he was entitled to behave towards Rachel as he did. Among all the other revelations that came to light during his trial, we learned that Joe had accused Rachel of being a bad mother to the point of being rough with her children.

What was worse was that, once he had chipped away at her self-esteem with his lies and his infidelity, he tried to convince her of it herself. I just could not understand how the girl we knew and loved so well could be portrayed in such a light; it just did not seem possible. She was not perfect, just like I am not perfect, and I have made mistakes throughout my life that I would rectify if I could. But in all my life I have never consciously done any harm to anyone, and Rachel was the same.

I, or anybody else that ever knew or met Rachel, would know what a brilliant mother she really was and I can only imagine the torture she was put through with the constant and persistent accusations she had to endure for God knows how long. Joe would paint a totally inaccurate picture of his wife for anyone who would care to listen, and I know how devious he was at creating the very image he wanted people to have of her, when it was really he who had all of the problems. When it began to emerge what Rachel had been subjected to and how she had suffered, I had thoughts about her murder that I cannot believe even entered my head. I try my best not to let that anger be any part of my thoughts but I find it a daily struggle. I have to keep remembering that no one can hurt Rachel any longer. Since Rachel's death, I have been told by her friends how on numerous occasions Joe was verbally abusive and disrespectful to Rachel in front of them. This causes me great anguish and sadness, and I only wish I'd known at the time. I had never heard Rachel bad-mouth Joe in any way. She loved him so much and could see no wrong in him; she never could.

Their relationship was certainly not equal in this regard. He seemed to think he owned her, but because his life with his wife did not satisfy him, he felt he needed more. I think somehow he blamed her for the lack of feelings he had for her at this time. It is evident he felt he needed more stimulation and excitement than Rachel could provide him, and as we know now he tried to fill this need with extramarital affairs. I have no doubt in my mind he will never find what he thinks he needs. I am firmly convinced that marriage would never fill this need and would not change him. I hope that he never gets the opportunity to repeat what he did to Rachel to any woman ever again. No amount of tears and sorrow will ever heal the permanent wounds he has inflicted on everyone who knew and loved Rachel.

I cannot help thinking of how different her life would have been if she had met and fallen in love with somebody else, somebody decent who would have loved her in return and given her the life she really deserved. I know she would have made the right person very happy, and life could have been so different for her, and for the rest of us. For some reason that only God knows, it was not to be; Rachel gave her heart to one who did not possess a heart, and we all know how dismally all of her love and efforts to be a good wife and mother failed in his eyes. Ultimately her husband turned out to be her executioner, chipping away at her as he did before killing her. I cannot imagine a greater evil than what was done to Rachel. I do my very best not to think of him, but it is a cross I carry now and every day of my life.

There have been many different parts of the whole ordeal that I have found particularly hard to bear, but being part of the trial of Rachel's murderer was one of many nightmares that you would not wish on your worst enemy. It brought to light a Joe O'Reilly that we knew nothing about, a Joe O'Reilly it still seems so hard to understand. I had always accepted him as being the person he appeared to be and I was so wrong. I was completely taken in by him. We have been exposed to a side of human nature we had never known and we have to be thankful that, for most of our lives, we were unaware of its existence. The upsetting part for us is that Rachel never had a chance. She could never have done the right thing in the eyes of Joe, and that had nothing to do with Rachel. I wish we could have let her know that she was the best person she could have been, and that none of what she was experiencing was her fault. What should have been the happiest days of her life were ruined long before her murder. At one stage during the trial, I just could not understand how the girl we knew and loved so well could be portrayed in such a light, it just did not seem possible. I no longer have to wonder. I still do not know the whys but I have come to learn that is just how it is.

I hope with all my heart that her horrific death will not have been in vain, and that there will come a change in the law whereby women are better protected from abusive partners. I hope that murders like Rachel's are not allowed to happen so frequently, and if, God forbid, they do happen, that the balance changes in favour of the victims, not the perpetrators.

It is now over four years since our Rachel was murdered, and it will soon be our fifth Christmas without her. Last Christmas was the hardest for me so far. The pain is unbearable. Sometimes, to distract myself, I get through the bad nights trying to work out a plan of how I could run away. Though I know this is not an option, in my darkest times I need some outlet from the stress and tension that is dominating my life. I long for peace and normality once again, and I hope to God I will find it soon. My fear is that I may never do so, because I now feel as though I am a different person. I have always been very happy with my lot in life. I have always felt blessed, and my family are, and always will be, the most important thing to me, which is why Rachel's murder has changed me for ever.

Part of that change is that I carry Rachel's spirit with me every day, because she is no longer here to share it herself. That was taken from her, just like her right to tell her side of the story was brutally taken. I give thanks that she had such a strong spirit of goodness, and her bubbly personality was what people noticed when they first met her, and what they remember her for today. It was only after she was murdered we all realized that happy sparkle that was her very essence had been crushed a long time before she was murdered. I know she will always be remembered by those who loved her as the kind of person she really was. She was everything you would ever want in a daughter – happy, loving and so confident. I often think of the beautiful, loving little girl we were so lucky to have had in our lives, and I remember so fondly the different stages of life we had with her as she grew up.

I feel strongly about telling Rachel's story, as I now know it. The trial gave me an insight into what she must have gone through for years before she was eventually murdered. I want to shed light on that story, her story, to undo the lies that Joe told about her, and to destroy his picture of Rachel that was so very far from the truth. As Joe so often said himself, 'I want to tell you this myself, as I do not want you to hear it from someone else' – only this time, it will be the beginning of the true story of Rachel's life.

1. A Beautiful Child

From the very start, Rachel captured our hearts. We have five adopted children, three boys and two girls: Declan and Paul first, then Rachel, our first girl, Ann, her sister, and last but not least our youngest son, Anthony. The fact that they were adopted and that we were blessed with having such a big family makes all our children hugely special to us. The babies were all about six weeks old when we adopted them with the exception of Rachel, who had contracted a virus. Although she had recovered from it well herself, she remained a carrier for it, and so we had to wait before she could leave the hospital and come home with us. I remember clearly the first day we met her – she was in a cot in the ward and she put her tiny arms out to

Jim. That was the way she was to remain, always so affectionate. Part of his sorrow is that her great love is now no longer part of our lives. Jim says he will always remember her as the little girl out of the fairy-tale books, like Heidi or Alice in Wonderland. She always did look so beautiful in her pretty little dresses with her hair shining like silk, silver white in the sun, and her beautiful tanned skin as brown as a nut.

Rachel was a beautiful baby, a lively toddler and grew into the most beautiful, capable, enthusiastic child, whose many friends from her early days will testify to her caring and loyalty, even when she was so young. One of the most vivid memories Jim and I hold of Rachel is of one day when she was just a baby and was toddling from the kitchen to the front room and back. At one stage, I became aware that she was out of sight and had gone very quiet. I rushed to the sitting room to discover her trying to climb up the chimney. She must have gotten as far as her head and her shoulders before she came back down, as she was completely black with soot, and her beautiful hair was completely obscured by soot, and her eyes just seemed to leap out of her little black face. She was having a go at getting up there again when I found her. I will never forget the job I had trying to get her cleaned up again.

Afterwards, she made several attempts at repeating her exploration of the chimney before she finally realized that it had been blocked up. It is one of the memories that the rest of her siblings still laugh about, as they have all heard that story many times through the years, as had Rachel herself.

Rachel was to bounce with such energy and enthusiasm throughout her short life. She always had this inexhaustible energy and would put her heart and soul into everything that she did, even when she was very young. One day, she came home from primary school and announced that she wanted to play the harp. You can imagine our re-action to such a small child picking such an unusual instrument! Apparently, a nun had told her she was good at it, so she'd taken a notion that she wanted to take lessons at school. There was just no dissuading her, but that was typical of Rachel. She loved it, practised hard and was very good at it. This would have been when Rachel was very young, only about seven years of age, a time when she was very much involved in gymnastics as well. I used to drive from one side of the city to the other, from Glasnevin to Muckross Park and sometimes to Chapelizod or Palmerstown, attending gymnastic competitions with Rachel. I often thought as I watched her practise that her joints seemed to be made of rubber.

It was beautiful to see her perform. She also enjoyed swimming and had done since she was about two and a half: she could swim effortlessly at this stage. When she was a young teenager, Rachel started doing shot-put, and I was concerned that she would build up large muscles in her arms, which mightn't look too good — but things like that didn't concern Rachel. She was also a keen badminton player, and it was a sport that Jim and all of the kids played in a local club. I tried it myself, but I couldn't ever really get the hang of it! Rachel continued to enjoy all sports and became very successful at them. From music to sport, she had an interest in everything — harp, guitar, singing and swimming, she was brilliant at all of them. Nothing would surprise you with Rachel, and she was the same her whole life: in April 2004, Rachel and her softball team friends entered *The Guinness Book of Records* for the world's longest softball match, which was held over a whole weekend in Templeogue. She was instrumental in the organization of the event and was thrilled when they broke the existing record — all of their hard work had paid off.

One of my clearest memories of Rachel's childhood years was when she got a new bike from Santa. I think she would have been about seven years old. It was a shiny new red bike with a basket on the front and a carrier on the back; she was thrilled with it. When the children were small, we had a small seven-seater minibus. The seats at the back used to fold down, and I could put the pram and all the bikes into it, and we often used to go down to Wicklow on summer days and have picnics by a stream, where the kids would play happily for hours.

The kids always loved to be outdoors, so we'd go out with them all throughout the year. One cold, dry, sunny Sunday afternoon a few weeks after Christmas, Jim and I put the three bikes in the mini-bus and took them all out to the Phoenix Park. The kids all set out cycling along in front of us on little paths that were far enough in from the roadway to be safe, and they were having a wonderful time. Declan, Paul and Rachel were cycling along, and I was pushing Ann along in the buggy. The kids loved the freedom and openness of the park, and would race each other up and down the pathways. They were used to seeing real cycle races held there, as Jim used to be a racing cyclist himself. He always loved and had a great interest in the sport and still does to this day. He passed a little of that interest on to the children when they were small. That day, we had been out for almost an hour and were on our way back to the car when all of a sudden Rachel took off, fearlessly leaving the path. She went tearing down a grassy hill straight across a very busy road with cars flashing by. I will never forget the fright we got that day; it was a miracle she was not killed.

The following summer, when we lived in Glasnevin Park, there was a big green out in front of our house encircled by a fairly quiet road. The children were allowed to cycle on the path, but I would always keep an eye on them as I used to sit knitting in our front room, which overlooked the green. One day, I noticed Rachel cycling very fast around the roadway, flying around the green with her eyes closed. I couldn't believe how dangerous it was, and how easily it could have ended in tragedy. She was not allowed to use her bike for a week after, and I don't think she repeated that stunt again. I can remember closing my eyes as a child and trying to navigate my way as far as I could without having to open them. I never did it on a bike, though, probably because by the time I had a bike I had the sense not to. All in all, though, the world Rachel grew up in was a much safer time, and we enjoyed a simpler way of life. They really were happy, carefree days for her, spent playing out with her friends, and it is something that has been lost to our grandchildren, which is a terrible shame.

*

When we were living at that house, Jim's eldest brother, Kevin, lived just a few doors up the road from us. We were always a close family, with all the aunts, uncles and cousins in and out the whole time, and that's still true today. As a child, Rachel was very close to all of her family, and when Kevin came by, he used to lift her on to his knee and she would give him a big hug. He would then ask her who she loved best, and she would turn her back so Jim could not see her and she would point to Kevin and mouth the word 'You' to him. Kevin used to get a great kick out of that!

We visited all of Rachel's aunts and uncles the day of her First Holy Communion, which I had been so looking forward to. I had made her dress and knit a cardigan, with socks and a bag to match, with yarn so fine that it was almost like a cobweb. I will never forget how excited she was that day as we saw all the family, and, to add to the excitement, Rachel's aunt Lucy was home on holiday from Australia and was staying with us. It was really a wonderful day.

Family and friends have always been a big part of life both in our house and on holidays. When Rachel was growing up, we used to go away with six or seven more families every Hallowe'en weekend to country cottages in various parts of Ireland. The children were sometimes well over twenty in number and always had a ball. The crowd, adults and children alike, would go for long hikes during the daytime and then have a gathering in a different one of the cottages each night. Each year, we were sure to put on something special for the children, and they would all dress up for the Hallowe'en party. Rachel loved these times and used to look forward to them so much. No matter what she decided to dress up as, she always looked beautiful. Every photograph of her on those weekends makes me feel so sad – she was so happy back then, and we felt she had a wonderful future ahead of her.

I feel the same when my mind goes back to how Rachel always loved her birthdays. She would be so excited at having all of her friends to her party. I would give her a number of people she could have over, between her school friends and her friends she'd play with near by. Every time, there would be double the number arriving than the number she was given – you could bet on it. She was so popular and had so many friends; her personality drew people to her even then.

Our family was the centre of our lives, and my parents' house was a place that all of our children knew very well. It was where we would all meet for family get-togethers, and all of our children were in constant contact with their cousins and relations; that was the kind of childhood Rachel had. Like us, Rachel was very family-orientated. She loved her grandparents and would have done anything for them, and they loved her in return. My own elderly mother was eighty-four years of age at the time Rachel died. Our family tried to keep the details of the circumstances of Rachel's death from her, but she found out from the television in the end. As soon as she heard how Rachel had died, and that I had found her, she said, 'Joe did it, he murdered her.' My brother Eugene was very shocked, and he told her not to be thinking such things. She would tell me herself much later that, as soon as she heard the news, she was convinced immediately that Joe had murdered Rachel. She was broken-hearted, and she never lived to see him convicted. That said, I am quite sure both my mam and my dad were looking down on us in the darkest hours of the trial and helped in getting justice for Rachel.

I have felt the loss of my parents so much through all of this horror and I miss the support that only your parents can give. Sometimes I am quite sure they are instrumental in the people who come up to us to offer their sympathy and support. I have often thought how just like my parents they are, decent, salt-of-the-earth people who just want to help. I am from a large family of nine, and each one of my siblings has been such a great support in whatever way they could be during our time of distress and difficulty.

Jim's family was an equally important part of our lives when the children were small, and are still today. Jim comes from a family of five: Lucy, his only sister, was the eldest; then Kevin, his brother who used to live near by; Jim was the one in the middle, followed by his brothers Tom and John. Jim's dad, Jimmy Senior, died before we were married and never had the pleasure of seeing any of his sons married or any of his grandchildren. His mother Ina was just sixty-six when she died of heart trouble but she was alive for the weddings and the births of Kevin's three children, some of Tom's and she was alive when we adopted Declan, Paul and Rachel. Rachel was still only a baby when she died, but we were so glad Granny Callaly had met all of them and had been in their lives.

I still look back on Rachel's life and think about the joy she brought to us. I feel an indescribable sadness at every cross word we ever had throughout her short life. We did have our differences, like any mother and daughter, but thank God not many, though I wish we never had any at all. I wish I could wipe out any cross word that went between us. Unfortunately, it does not work like that, and I love and miss her so much that it tears me apart. I thank God she knew how much she was loved and, in turn, I know how much she loved us. Above all else, we mourn all the things that we can no longer share with Rachel and her two children as they go through life without their mother by their sides.

I consider myself lucky to be able to always treasure those memories of her childhood, but I am saddened at the thought of all the experiences that were denied to Rachel, and all the memories of her children growing up that she will never have. Knowing that the little time she was allowed on this earth was so tainted by the treachery that was going on in her own home makes it much harder. The accusations she was confronted with must have left her feeling completely bewildered. No young mother should be surrounded by constant scrutiny, and I have no doubt what she was subjected to must have affected her confidence. She would not have experienced the simple pleasure of bringing up her own two children as any normal girl would, without constant criticisms and negative undercurrents going on around her. Rachel had her children's interests at heart at all times – they were her children, after all. We all have our own ways of bringing up our children, and she had every right to do the same, but unfortunately, unbeknownst to us, she was not allowed her basic right to mother her children as she saw fit, and I have no doubt that the criticism she suffered must have caused her a great deal of pain. I only wish we had known and could have reassured her.

My greatest wish in life is that her two little children will grow up in the knowledge of how much she loved them and that they were her reason for living. I pray that some day they will feel and know what a beautiful person their mother was. I sincerely hope that they both possess their mother's wonderful spirit, because it will be the most important thing they could have to help them through life. They have lost more than any of us, and to be betrayed by their own father as they have been is the ultimate act of evil that can befall any child.

Whenever I spent time with Rachel and the children, I often thought how she just loved to be with them – they were so happy. She never seemed to want anything more than to be with her family. Rachel's greatest interest in life was being a mother and a wife. She might not have been the greatest cook, but she had a lot more to do in her family than a lot of mothers, as she raised her two children and literally did everything about the house and gardens herself with no support from Joe at all. Rachel had said to me on many occasions that Joe was never home, but I never realized until she was gone that it was literally the truth. When my children were very young, Jim worked very long hours, too, and I presumed that Rachel was in a similar situation. She felt the job was taking up far too much of his time, and he did not get to spend enough time at home. I wish I had realized the extent of the problem then so that I could have been more supportive.

Joe, meanwhile, concentrated on telling stories about her that weren't true and manipulated every situation to make her look as bad as he could to his family and friends, which we learned through email evidence presented during the trial. Who could pass such scrutiny at every level and come out with flying colours? No one is good at everything, and in normal circumstances someone's faults would balance out with their gifts. Rachel's circumstances were definitely not normal; her husband was having a separate life with another partner, he wasn't honest or open with Rachel about any part of it and he seemed to think he had the perfect right to live as he wished, staying out to be with his lover whenever he thought fit, leaving his wife to cope whatever way she could. I often think of the beautiful big garden they had and how sad and alone Rachel must have felt at never having the company of her children's father, which would have made their lives so happy and enjoyable for all of them. They might have enjoyed as happy a family life as we had, and their children could have had the kind of carefree childhood that had made Rachel the loving person she was. But the worst part is that Joe made it clear that he felt in no way responsible for any part of the situation. He laid the blame for everything at Rachel's feet.

2. Rachel's First – and Only – Love

In 1987, when Rachel was thirteen years old, we emigrated to Perth in Western Australia, as there was a recession on here in Ireland. We thought that Australia would offer more opportunities for the children, but we thought long and hard before we decided to sell the home that we had lived in since we were first married to go and start afresh. Jim felt that if the house was still here that it would have been a pull on us if things got difficult, and we would always wonder if we had tried hard enough to settle. It was not an easy thing, trying to sell property at that time, and the prices had dropped considerably, but we sold the house eventually. We packed up all of our belongings and sent them ahead of us by container ship.

On the way over to Perth, we stopped off in Bangkok for a few days to break the journey for the children, and to take in the sights of the city. It was a great thing to do, as the kids got to experience so much of the completely different culture of Thailand. We had the services of a guide, who would come to our hotel each morning to collect us, and I still wonder what she must have thought when she would see my eyes each morning almost closed from crying. She would not have understood that we were emigrating and had just left our parents, siblings and all of our friends behind. It must have seemed so strange to her. She took us to see many of the best-known sights of Bangkok, and some of the temples, which were extremely beautiful. As we came to the end of our day visiting the temples, Anthony refused to once again take off his shoes as you were supposed to do. We had to remove them for him and carry him through the remainder of the temples. It was a beautiful experience, and the sense of calm about them had a spiritual quality to it. I would love to return and see them all again.

Another day, we were taken down on the river to see the floating markets, with people selling their wares and produce from very long, narrow and flimsy-looking boats. The atmosphere was magic, with the crowds chattering and bartering in a scene so different from our Moore Street in Dublin — the people seemed so gentle and helpful, and they worked so hard, but so cheerfully. We were amazed at the things for sale that were piled up in such fragile boats, but the sellers made a difficult job look so easy as they took it in their stride. Rachel would soak up all of these experiences, and she just enjoyed every moment of it. She would look after Anthony and loved showing him all the new sights. Later that same day, when we were taken further down the river, passing wooden houses on stilts all along the banks, the Thai children would jump off the balconies of the houses into the river. At first I was afraid they would drown, only to see them emerge full of laughter and excitement. I remember thinking that they had so little but were so happy, that they could teach us a lot. Further down the river still, we got out of the boats to visit a small zoo. Rachel held Anthony as we watched snake charmers handle enormous big snakes, and I can still see her laughing at the antics of the monkeys. I know that if I ever do go to visit again, Rachel will be there with me.

Once we arrived in Australia, we weren't completely without our family, as Jim's only sister, Lucy, had gone to Australia when she was fifteen years old to enter the Dominican Sisters and was enjoying a very happy life in Western Australia. We decided to settle in Perth, as that was where Lucy, now Sister Declan, lived. Though some of the children found it hard at first, Rachel took to the whole experience like a duck to water and just seemed to blossom there. I have a picture in my mind from those days, as she cycled up the road on her new bike in the sunshine. I knew at the time that it was one of those memories I would never lose.

The children settled into the local school where Lucy was a teacher – she even taught our Declan English while we were there. They got on very well and became very involved in their classes. One day, Rachel came home and told us she had joined a woodworking class. She said that she found it really interesting and was very enthusiastic about it. I still remember the little table she brought home after a few weeks of classes. She had finished it off perfectly and was so proud of it. But all of this was par for the course with Rachel; it was the harp lessons all over again. We laughed the day she came home from school and announced that she had joined the school's brass band. Jim smiled and asked her would she have any time left for sleep? She seemed to pack in three times more into her short life than anyone else. She really was *living* her life!

She celebrated her fourteenth birthday while we

were there, and rather than the parties she'd had indoors in Glasnevin Park, this time she got to have a very different party — a pool party in our own back garden. She really enjoyed it and was surrounded by many new friends. Shortly afterwards, she got a part-time job in a deli on Saturdays, quite close to where we lived. The hours were good, and she enjoyed the independence it gave her. Later on, she came home all excited because she had been offered a new job for much more money, but this time in a video rental shop. She would have looked older than her fourteen years at the time, and we didn't like the idea of her working in the evenings. She was very upset when we would not let her take it and couldn't see any reason why she couldn't. She was a very trusting person, and the idea that there might be people out there who would try to take advantage of her would never have occurred to her. In the end, of course, she got over her disappointment and continued to work in the deli. When we were in Australia, Rachel never seemed to have spare time. Her life was always so full of such varied activities that she hardly stopped for breath. The weather in Perth was fantastic, as the breeze coming in from the coast always kept the temperatures from getting too overpowering, and Rachel was in her element getting out in the fresh air. She went on to make many friends in Perth, some of whom she kept in contact with up to the time she died.

As it turned out, we were to return to Ireland after just one year. Jim had developed and built up his own plumbing business in Ireland and he thought that, by moving to Australia, our children would not have to work quite as hard as he always had to make a good living, that they would have an easier life. I suppose that the grass is always greener – we learned that, no matter where you live, if you want something badly enough in this life you must work hard to achieve it. He and I had made a pact that if either of us didn't settle, we would pack it in and go home, so when Jim found it hard to adjust, that's what we did. Working life in Australia was very different to Ireland. I guess that if Jim had been fifteen years younger, he might have adjusted, but, as that was not the case, after a year living in Perth, we decided life in Ireland would suit us as a family better. After much soul-searching and discussion, we decided to come back home again.

We made the return trip home into the holiday of a lifetime for the family. Jim and I felt it would probably be the last time that the older children would want to do a family holiday, so we made the absolute most of it. First, we visited Sydney and spent several days seeing the sights. We then spent a week in Queensland, where Jim and the children swam out on to the Great Barrier Reef. I can still remember looking at an unbelievable scene of tropical fish of every colour, shape and size swimming between the coral, with Jim, Declan, Paul and Rachel along with many others swimming amongst them as Ann, Anthony and myself watched them from a glass-bottomed boat. We had lunch on the boat, and the children had a great day.

We spent the last three weeks in the United States – a week on the island of Oahu in Hawaii, where the children had a great time surfing and swimming on Waikiki beach. We visited the volcanoes on the island – some of the craters were massive in size – and the lads got to see the set where the TV series *Hawaii 5–0* was made. It wasn't any way as glamorous as it looked on TV, but the kids were thrilled to see it. We took a tour of the Del Monte plantation, where we were shown around and given pineapples to taste – before that, Del Monte was just a name on a tin, but now when I see it I can picture the exotic location, which was such a beautiful spot.

Somewhere else that will always stay in my mind is Pearl Harbor. There is a huge memorial built right beside where one of the big ships went down during the Japanese attack. You can still actually see the ship lying on the ocean floor right next to the names and ages of all the sailors who lost their lives carved into the marble memorial. It gave me a very eerie feeling and a sense of the men's spirits being there to this day. Some of them had been little more than boys. None of the bodies had been removed, as it was decided back then to let them rest where they were, but they will never be forgotten.

From Hawaii, we flew to Los Angeles, where we were met by my sister Sindy. We spent a couple of days in Disneyland, which was one of the highlights of our trip. The kids really had a great time trying out as many of the rides as they could. At night the Disney characters danced along to music under flickering lights. It is hard to describe the atmosphere, but it was just magic. Jim and I were always so glad we had gone there as a family; it is one of our happiest memories. We then drove to Desert Hot Springs to visit my brother Ray, his wife, Denise, and their family. We visited the Mammoth Lakes District, which is a spectacular elevated mountain area surrounded by lakes. As we drove up through the snow-covered mountains, it was such a big contrast to the dry, arid heat of the desert, which had a subtle beauty all of its own. We arrived at a ski resort just as the season ended, though the slopes were still covered in snow. Small furry creatures like squirrels darted around and would watch us from a safe distance – the kids were fascinated by them. It looked like a different world, with beautiful log cabins and ski lodges dotted about the scenery.

We also visited Yosemite National Park, where the waterfalls were spectacular. We could hardly believe the size of the ancient sequoia trees, some of the roots of which you could drive a car through, the base of the trees were so wide. Eventually, we went back down into the desert, driving through Death Valley to Las Vegas. The heat rippled upward in Death Valley so strongly that it felt like you could reach out and touch it with your hand, as if it were a living thing. Initially, I had not been keen on visiting Las Vegas, and we were overwhelmed by our first sight of the bright lights and the throngs of people that never seemed to diminish. We spent a few nights in The Golden Nugget, which was a palatial hotel, and had a wonderful time. We took in as many of the sights as we could, but just barely scratched the surface. Despite my reservations, I'd actually like to visit again, as there were a lot of sights and shows that we could not visit with the children.

The last stop on the tour was San Francisco, where we saw all the sights including Fisherman's Wharf, the Golden Gate Bridge and the island of Alcatraz. The former prison was an interesting but very unsettling part of the trip, and I still remember the strange feeling I had standing on the island and looking over the bay to Fisherman's Wharf and the very lively coastline on either side of it. It gave me an amazing sense of the alienation the prisoners must have felt, being able to see and even hear life on the mainland. I could not help but feel how the stark contrast must have added to their plight. It was something I just did not want to think about, being imprisoned on a bare rock, but yet being able to hear and see people enjoying freedom on the lively bay-side opposite.

San Francisco was our last port of call on that holiday, and we were all very excited about coming back home to Ireland once again. When we arrived in Dublin airport we were met by a huge number of our family and friends. It was comforting to see all of the familiar faces that we knew would be there for us as we started life again in Ireland, and we realized how much we had come to rely on them being part of our daily lives. It was in part because we were so close to our extended family and friends that we were so happy to return.

We all have amazing memories of that once-in-a-lifetime holiday when we were all together. We always felt that, maybe one day, Rachel would be the one in the family to return to Australia to live, but she met Joe at a very young age, and her fate was sealed.

When we returned home, Rachel got a part-time job on Saturdays at a Peter Marks hair salon. It was here that she first met Paula, who would remain a great friend until the time that Rachel died. Rachel loved the work and chatting with all the people who came in and was very happy there until she developed a bad case of dermatitis from the chemicals and colourings. It got so bad she could no longer work there, and she then took a part-time job at Shay's, our local newsagents, while she was at college. But soon after, she got a job in Arnott's department store. It was here that she met Joe when she was just seventeen years old; he was working in the haberdashery department full-time and was about a year and a half older than Rachel. Like any romance between young teenagers, it wasn't very serious to start with, and though we were happy that she was happy, we didn't pay it much attention. As a result, we don't know much about those early days and what went on, but I have learned since that he set out from the beginning to do all he could to win her over. Soon, it was clear that she was mad about him, and she made no secret of it. Even though she only worked there one day per week, and didn't get all that much time with him as she was still in college, once she started to date Joe, her heart was his for ever. They did all the normal things young couples do – going to the cinema and socializing with their many friends – and we had no reason to worry. As it turned out, she never went out with anybody else; she was very much in love, and he was all she ever wanted out of life.

It would never have entered Rachel's head that the person she loved so much was not what he appeared to be, but of course it never occurred to us, either. On reflection, I could never really take to him, a feeling which I still to this day cannot explain or put into words. As you do when it comes to your children's partners, I didn't dwell on it and got on with family life. Despite never warming to him, I must admit I could never have imagined what lay underneath his calm, charming and polite exterior. All I knew was that Rachel adored him, and he seemed to us to make her happy, which is the most important thing. Rachel was completely in love and thought that whatever Joe said was gospel.

I always felt that he considered himself to be an authority on everything, and he managed to convince Rachel he was too. Back then, though, I was just concerned with Rachel's happiness. It would be years before I fully understood how manipulative and controlling he really was.

Early on in their relationship, Rachel wanted to go back to Australia for a holiday. When she had first met Joe, he told her that he had lived in Australia and that he held Australian citizenship. I was very surprised then when I heard that some problem was preventing him from going with Rachel on a holiday there, but Joe maintained that he could not enter Australia any more. It didn't seem to add up, but Rachel believed his story and went ahead by herself, visiting her old friends and Aunt Lucy once again. She had a fantastic holiday, spending time in Perth and further north in Tardun, where her Aunt Lucy was then teaching at an agricultural school.

Though little things like this incident register in your mind at the time, that was more or less the extent of it. It didn't feel right, but I certainly never attached anything sinister to it, and if Rachel didn't volunteer to discuss something, I wouldn't have questioned her. Hindsight is a great thing, and

I wish I had spoken to her about it. After Rachel was murdered, my friend Val reminded me that shortly after Rachel returned from Australia, I confided in her that, when Rachel spoke about the trip in front of Joe, telling me all about the things she did and the people she met, he would give her a look that would silence her. Apparently, I told Val that I found it very odd, and that I couldn't imagine what the problem was. I remember one such incident when Joe was standing in our kitchen, and Rachel was excitedly telling us about the holiday. I noticed that when their eyes met, she looked at the floor and changed the subject immediately. I sensed that something was not quite right and I felt very uneasy about it. I have no recollection of telling the story to Val, even though I remember the incident itself very well. I can only think that it must have worried me to have voiced my concern. I never heard Rachel discuss or talk about her trip in Joe's presence after that.

The summer just before Rachel turned twenty, there was a disagreement in the house over Rachel putting on the potatoes for the dinner. Although she would have done anything else you asked of her – she would have walked to Cork and back on an errand for you – she had never been fond of cooking. An argument started about which of the children did which chores around the house and ended when Rachel went out and said she was not coming back. I did not think she meant it, as the argument seemed so unimportant, but we were devastated when we realized she really was not coming back. I felt at the time that Joe was behind her decision, and I remember thinking that he was a negative influence on her. I said to her that if it did not work out, she was not to feel awkward, that she was just to come home. I told Rachel that her home would always be open to her and that she could come back anytime she wanted to, for any reason, but that Joe was not welcome. I never spoke negatively about Joe to Rachel after that. The move didn't upset our relationship in the long term, and Rachel and I were back on good terms soon after. We continued to be very close, and, over time, Joe was welcomed and included in family occasions.

To Rachel, Joe was everything he appeared to be, and she fell for him, hook, line and sinker. When Rachel called us to give us the news of her engagement, though I was glad for her as she was so happy, I still had an uneasy feeling about Joe. Once again, a friend recalled me saying that I hoped he was the right one for her and that she was not making a mistake.

When they got engaged after having been together for about four years, I tried as best I could for Rachel's sake to include Joe in the family, and, as the years passed, I made sure to treat him just the same as I did my sons' wives. He was included in everything we did as a family, and he seemed like a decent, helpful sort of a person – and I was determined to be positive about him and their engagement. He appeared to be the kind of a person who always seemed to say the right thing and, on the face of it, always tried to be helpful. Looking back, you could just as easily have said that he was charming but manipulative, someone who always said what people wanted to hear.

To all outward appearances, he was friendly and charming, but I know now how he really felt about us. After Rachel died, I was bewildered to learn his true feelings of venom towards my family and to see how the hatred he had shown Rachel would be transferred on to us – myself and Ann in particular. One of the most upsetting things about Rachel's murder is that I know now that my instincts about Joe were correct and I can't help but wonder what I could have done differently to prevent what happened. No matter what scenario I imagine, I still have not come up with an answer.

3. Becoming a Family: Rachel's Dreams Come True

When Rachel and Joe got engaged, they were working hard to save for a deposit on a house. She was having dinner at our house one evening and was browsing through the ads in the *Evening Herald* when she saw a house for sale in Aulden Grange in Santry, not too far away from us. She was so excited, and soon after they made an offer on the house, which was then accepted. I often think if she had not sold and left that house for the bigger one they later moved into that she would still be alive today as the new house in The Naul was in a very quiet and secluded area, and the one they had left was semi-detached and in a busy estate.

Rachel moved on with life and it was a very happy time for her. After a good while working and saving hard to get the deposit on the house in Santry, they were thrilled to finally achieve their goal just a year before they were married. I remember how happy she was back then: life was good and she was so looking forward to their future together. Once the house was secured, Rachel then started organizing the wedding. As with a lot of brides, the planning seemed to take over her life, and she enjoyed every minute of it. She went to so much trouble picking the venue, choosing the menus and getting a beautiful wedding cake made in Kilkenny. She wanted everything to be perfect and knew exactly what she wanted for her dress. She loved searching for just the right one and finally found one she was happy with, only to go through the same again with the bridesmaid dresses. She then planned and organized their dream honeymoon to Kenya. She was so capable and thorough about everything, from the invitations down to the flowers, that it was a joy to see her so excited about their big day. In the end, it belied all the months of hard work she had put into it. She had successfully done it all herself, and we were so proud of her.

Joe wasn't very involved in much of the wedding planning, but I suppose that most men would be the same. It was a happy family time nonetheless, and we made a point of meeting Joe's mother a couple of months before the wedding. Jim and I took her, Joe and Rachel out for a meal, and I had the impression that she was a pleasant person. More importantly, I was glad to see firsthand how well Rachel seemed to get on with her. After this, though, I never got to know her well at all, but I appreciated that she seemed so supportive of Rachel.

The morning of the wedding, I went into Rachel's bedroom and I got a strong urge to get into the bed beside her, something I had not felt since she was grown. Looking back, Rachel could never have known the feelings that I had, and I still cannot explain it to myself, but I was overwhelmed by trying to protect her. It felt like Rachel was embarking on a new and very important phase in her life. It was such a big step for her. All the time, I was hoping with all my heart that she would be happy. We lay there chatting for a while, but then we got up as the bridesmaids were coming to have breakfast in our house. After breakfast, the beautician arrived, and I became engrossed in all of the excitement that was going on with Rachel and all the bridesmaids getting their make-up done and getting dressed. Then they all went around to Paula, Rachel's friend in the salon, to have their hair done, and the hairstyles were beautiful. Rachel looked stunning with an up-style hairdo, with soft curls around her face.

It was a bright day, quite mild for April, and I will always hold dear the memory of how she looked that day. I had often heard it said that a girl made a 'radiant bride', and indeed I had seen many, many brides in my time, but never one as radiant and beautiful as Rachel. It was as if she was lit up on the inside. I remember Ann saying to me, 'If I look half as beautiful on my wedding day, I will be happy.' Her bridesmaids were lovely as well, and everything flowed right into place for her as the day turned out just as she'd hoped and planned. When we all arrived at the church, I saw Joe and thought how well he looked. Rachel never seemed happier than she did on that morning.

As you'd expect, the photographer was whizzing about taking this shot and that shot before Rachel entered the church for the ceremony. Jim was very emotional as he led our beautiful daughter up the aisle and handed her over to Joe, the man who was to cherish and protect her from then on. It was a beautiful and a very moving occasion for Jim and me, as Rachel was the first of our five children to be married.

There was only one thing that didn't go to plan that morning, as far as I can remember. After the ceremony, when the photographer had finished all of the formal photos both outside and inside the church, she discovered that she had not taken a picture of Rachel and her dad as he led her up the aisle to give her away. They made a big joke out of it, removing Rachel's wedding ring, and Jim leading her back up the aisle again. Nobody seemed to think anything of it at the time, but it definitely sent a shiver down my spine. I could not explain it, but it was as if we were trying to undo what had been done, to turn back time. It just gave me a feeling that it was somehow an unlucky thing to have happened. I can't explain why, and nobody else seemed concerned or to take any notice of it, so I tried not to think of it and went on with the celebrations. I wonder now if it wasn't just another cloud on the horizon, a sign of what was to come.

The wedding day went brilliantly, and Joe and Rachel seemed so happy. Her face just shone with love right through the day. I can still remember her smile as she danced in Joe's arms and hear her happy laughter as she clowned about the dance floor with Myles and Lar, good friends of ours she had known since she was a baby. My mam and dad, Rachel's beloved grandparents, were there, something for which I will always be grateful, as my dad passed away quite suddenly not long after that. Thank God it was such a wonderful occasion for her, as, unbeknownst to any of us, she would not be happy for very long.

When the newlyweds returned from their Kenyan honeymoon, Jim, Ann, Anthony and I welcomed them home at the airport, and we went back to their house for some refreshments. I was surprised when Rachel didn't have much to say about it, particularly as it had taken so much planning and she was so looking forward to it. Normally, she would have been very enthusiastic about any new experience, particularly something as romantic as their honeymoon, but she explained that Joe had got the chickenpox while in Kenya and had been very ill for most of the trip. I felt so sorry for her that it was not as she had dreamed it was going to be, and I had no reason to doubt her explanation. She didn't let her disappointment show too much, and I know she was looking forward to married life, making a home and sharing it all with Joe. But I still do not know how Joe felt at that time, how the honeymoon really went or when he was to change, if indeed he did change at all.

After she married, Rachel was working in a solicitor's office, and her job there was going well.

Joe changed jobs several times during that early period, but each move was an improvement on his last position, so despite the upheaval, it was a very positive time for them. Rachel was always very supportive of him and helped him all she could, searching the Internet for suitable promotional opportunities for her husband, helping to prepare his curriculum vitae and encouraging him to move forward. I don't know who would have instigated the job changes, or whether it was Joe who wanted to keep moving forward in his career, but, for his part, Joe seemed to be a capable and hard-working man, and we were very pleased for them about how they were getting on.

Looking back, she had so much energy in those first few years of her marriage and she was so happy that she was every bit the Rachel we knew and loved, with the same enthusiasm she had all through her childhood. She was absolutely thrilled when she found out that she was pregnant for the first time. However, it turned out to be a very difficult pregnancy, and she was very sick the whole time she carried the baby. It really was unusually bad, and we did all we could to help. Then, when her first baby was born in March 2000, it had truly all been worthwhile. Her baby was so beautiful and looked so much like Rachel herself. I used to think that you could have been looking at Rachel herself as a baby. She was so happy and loved her baby to bits, as any young mother would.

Her first child was not yet one when Rachel became pregnant again. I will never forget how sick she was during this second pregnancy, even worse than the previous time. One day she rang me and was very upset. When I went up to the house, I could hardly believe how ill she was. She was so sick she could hardly hold her head up and she whispered to me, 'Mam, I just can't cope.' She looked so frightened. I reassured Rachel, staying with her some time, and then I brought my grand-child home with me while she took a rest and got some energy back. Many, many times I took her in to the Rotunda Hospital, and she was so weak and getting sick so much during that pregnancy that she had to be hospitalized on several different occasions. At one point, I was driving her to the hospital and was using the bus lane to get there as fast as I could. I was panicking because I thought she might go into early labour. We were stopped by a Garda, who took one look at Rachel and quickly ushered us on when he saw her condition. She really had a very tough time. When her second child was born in October of 2001, they were thrilled. Just as their first-born looked like Rachel, their second looked very like Joe's side of the family and was a happy, healthy baby.

With a new baby at home and a very energetic toddler to look after, it was not an easy time for Rachel. Having been so sick beforehand, she was run down by the time she came home from the hospital, and the stress took its toll. She was very tired in the first few months, and Joe was every bit the supportive father during that time. He worked a very short distance from where they were living then and he used to come home at lunchtime to take the youngest out in the buggy around the nearby green and get the baby off to sleep so Rachel would get a break. I thought a lot of him for doing that, as it was a special time in Rachel's life. Joe had appeared to be so good with his two children in the beginning. But his wife was also a brilliant parent, and not long after this would love and nourish their children with no support from her husband. Even with all the new experiences and emotions that come in the very early stages of being a new mother, Rachel was thinking ahead for her two children from the very start. She was full of hopes and dreams for them and all they would achieve, and I am so glad that I told her on many occasions what a great mother she was.

I also helped out when she needed a hand, and at

one stage, when her second child was only a few months old, Rachel asked me if I would babysit for them so as she and Joe could have an evening out together. So, I used to go up every Tuesday, and they would go to see a movie and have a bite to eat after. These weekly outings seemed to fizzle out after a bit, but I did not give it much thought at the time. On looking back, maybe the cracks were showing even then, but I just can't know for sure – you never know what's going on in someone else's marriage unless they tell you.

Rachel seemed happy with her two little children and had a very busy life. She made a lot of improvements to their house in Santry, including having a new kitchen fitted and new windows installed throughout the house, and finally she had a beautiful conservatory built on to the back of the house. Eventually, though, they started to think about moving to a bigger house somewhere else. I remember Rachel giving several reasons for their wanting to move: the property market was working in their favour, as they were lucky to have bought their house in Santry just before the prices had jumped so steeply, so they were in a good position by the time it came to moving up the property ladder.

It may seem totally odd, but one of the reasons for them wanting to move was so that Joe could have a separate room to house and display his collection of *Star Wars* memorabilia. Joe was a long-time *Star Wars* fanatic, and no matter where we went, Rachel would end up going through *Star Wars* merchandise and, nine times out of ten, ring Joe to ask him had he this figurine or that one. She never left without buying him something. She must have spent a fortune on memorabilia over the years, and I remember thinking on more than one occasion that she would be better off treating herself to something nice. But she never seemed to think of herself, it was always something for Joe or the children, but I never said anything as she seemed to be happy doing just that. She and Joe had looked into the possibility of converting the attic for his collection, but it was working out to be very costly and they decided that a move would make more sense, what with the children getting older. In hindsight, it would all be wasted effort.

House prices were rising by the week at that point in early 2003, and I remember that she had her eye on a house that was for sale in Donabate. She always loved the sea, and living by the sea would have been perfect for her and, she thought, for the children as well. Even now, I know she is there with me any time Jim and I are walking by the coast. In the end, the house in Donabate did not work out, and she then began talking about moving out to the country. I tried in every way I could think of to dissuade her, pointing out that it would be hard on Joe sitting in traffic twice a day, commuting in and out to work, but she said that Joe was as anxious as she was to move out of the city. I explained to her that there would be many years not too far away when she would have to ferry the children everywhere by car, and the big undertaking it would be every day just to get everyone to where they were supposed to go, but no matter what I came up with, it did not make any difference: she was quite positive and went ahead with the move. When they finally did move to The Naul and I saw how much she truly loved living there, I often felt guilty that I had ever tried to put her off – country living really suited her, and I was convinced that I had been completely wrong in my misgivings.

I remember the week they moved into the house called 'Lambay View', in Baldarragh, The Naul. Just a couple of days after they moved in, Ann and I called out to see Rachel. I had bought them a new garden table and chairs and I wanted to let her have the use of them straight away, as I thought it might be useful while they unpacked all their furniture. Ann and I got lost on the way out, going around in circles, and by the time we found the house it was late in the evening, after 8 p.m. if I remember rightly. When we arrived, Rachel was in the kitchen on her own, surrounded by boxes upon boxes of belongings not yet unpacked. I asked her where Joe and the children were and I can still picture her answering as she sat there. She explained that Joe had taken them to his mother's and he would stay there with them for a few days to give Rachel a chance to unpack and get the house liveable. There seemed to be something very vulnerable about her as she said it, and I was horrified at the notion that he would leave her there to do that all on her own. I could understand him wanting the two children to be occupied with something else while they tried to get everything unpacked, but when I asked Rachel why Joe hadn't just left them with his mother and then come back home to get the work done between them, she gave me some unconvincing reason that didn't make much sense. I did not want to push it, as she was clearly uncomfortable with the situation. Ann and I offered to stay and get some of the boxes unpacked, many of which Ann had helped her wrap and pack when she was moving from Santry, but she refused, explaining that her best friend, Jackie, was coming over from work to help and was going to stay the night. Rachel said they had plans to order in a Chinese and open a bottle of wine when they had finished, so I did not insist on staying, as I felt they would probably enjoy the evening together once the work was done. I was very glad Jackie was coming over, as I know she was always very supportive of Rachel and always helped any time she could. She worked as a nurse, and because she worked shifts, it would not be unusual for her to call out at different times of the day. All the same, I remember feeling very uneasy as I drove home that evening: there was something not quite right going on. I just felt that there was no reason that I could think of why Joe should not be there with Rachel. After all, this was a huge venture for them, setting up a home again in a new house, and it's well known how stressful moving can be. Somehow, the situation just did not seem normal. It was hard to know what to do for the best – do you intervene and risk being seen to be interfering? I didn't know what to think at all, and I confided my worries to Jim when I got home, who said he didn't know what to make of it, but that if she said that it was all right, we'd have to take her at her word.

Within a few months of their moving into Lambay View, Rachel organized to have everyone up to a barbecue as a house-warming party. She gave an open invitation to all the neighbours, her friends from her softball team, Joe's family and her own aunts, uncles and cousins, in addition to all of our immediate family. There was quite a crowd there that day, and as there was loads of room in the garden, Rachel had even hired a bouncy castle for the children. Needless to say, they had a ball and were really enjoying the bouncy castle, and Rachel had as much fun as they did, jumping and bouncing among them. I remember marvelling at her energy and enthusiasm that day – she looked like one of the children herself, so full of life.

We did not have any chat with Joe that day, and, as I look back, I realize he was keeping out of our way, but we didn't think it was too unusual, as it was typical enough for Joe to keep to himself. Even if it was an occasion with plenty of family around, Joe would always leave the company of the adults and play with the children. Any conversation we did have would be pleasant enough, but very general, never anything particularly personal about him. We came to accept that he just wasn't a great mixer, but, looking back, we never really got to know him at all.

After Rachel's death, some of her friends told us that, even though they would be invited out for a meal, it was not unusual for Joe to have his alone in front of the television, leaving his wife, children and the guests to have theirs in the kitchen without him. He would always seem either unable or unwilling to join the rest of the company. Looking back, I just don't know why Rachel put up with his behaviour. I now wonder what on earth she could have loved about him.

The big garden was one of the things that Rachel loved most about that house. It was a bit wild when they moved in, but she planned to get it back into shape so that the children could have the freedom of it. Jim gave her a present of some money to buy whatever she wanted for the house, so she decided she would buy a ride-on lawnmower for the garden. I can still see her bombing around the grass on it. She loved it, and I was very glad she had it as she was the one left to cut the grass, clip the hedges and generally keep the gardens in shape, which was quite a job for one person. When he rang the house to thank us for the gift, and I was the one he spoke to, I felt that the very offhand way of thanking us had been down to Rachel getting him to acknowledge the gift of money, and that she had needed to ask him to call.

Rachel was also busy, but busy with family life. Rachel loved doing a million different things at once, but keeping house with all the other demands of family life with two small children was a challenge for her. I think that she took on so many things that it got to be too much for her. Rachel was an agent for Avon cosmetics and for Tupperware, in addition to which she used to do a small amount of work at her home for her former boss. So between all that, looking after two energetic children, and what with the house and gardens to keep, she found it hard to keep the balance.

On top of her work at home, Rachel was very supportive to Joe's mother, Anne O'Reilly Senior. She tried to help her in every way she could, and I assumed that they were just as supportive to Rachel in return. When Rachel moved to The Naul, she told me how much Joe's mother had always wanted to move to the country herself. Rachel and Joe were even thinking of building a granny flat on to the side of the house to accommodate her. I felt this might be a bit stressful on Rachel, as I have always truly believed that every young couple is better off living their own life without constantly having the parents from either side around, but I did not voice my concerns as I didn't want to interfere in their plans.

The granny flat idea did not come to fruition, as it turned out, but later Rachel told me that she was actively looking for houses on the market that her mother-in-law could afford, something that took up a good bit of her time. In the end, it was Rachel who was instrumental in getting the house where Joe's mother now lives, and she even helped her to furnish it. Rachel brought her mother-in-law to buy all of her appliances, floor coverings and everything she needed for the new house. She also arranged for someone to lay the tiles and the floor coverings. Finally, Rachel successfully convinced her mother-in-law that she would not survive living in the country unless she learned to drive, and it was through Rachel's constant encouragement and help that Anne O'Reilly Snr set about getting her driver's licence. On the face of it, Rachel enjoyed a good relationship with her husband and her in-laws in those early years, or so we thought. At that time I had no idea about any problems between Rachel and Joe. And it was only when I heard the evidence at his trial – the emails that were read out that passed between Joe and Anne O'Reilly Jnr – that I became aware of their true feelings towards Rachel. Knowing all that Rachel had done for her mother-in-law from the very beginning made her betrayal of Rachel all the harder to take.

4. Remembering Family Times

I can only recall two occasions when Joe let his mask slip. One of them was on a day when Joe and Rachel had called into our house. The two of them were on their own as the two children were at school and crèche. As they were leaving, Joe started to poke fun at Rachel about her size. Jim and I were very surprised at Joe's behaviour, as we had never witnessed this side of him before. It was not being said in a jovial way, and we were caught off-guard by the insulting, cruel way he was speaking about his wife. Rachel did not answer him, but I could see she was very hurt. It was particularly cruel because, after her first child was born, Rachel had found it hard to shift the weight she had put on during the pregnancy. She really made a serious effort: she joined Weight Watchers and managed to get back to her normal size, but no sooner had she got back to normal than she became pregnant with her second child. This time around, it seemed much harder to lose the weight, which a lot of women find to be the case. On reflection, if she was being criticized by Joe about her pregnancy-related weight, on top of getting no support from him, we can only imagine how hard that must have been. I have never forgotten the way he looked at her that day, and his behaviour then was explained when I learned his true feelings.

The other occasion was the Christmas morning, 2003, the year before she died. All of our family – brothers, sisters, aunts, uncles, grandchildren, nieces and nephews – met in our house, as they do every Christmas morning. Rachel really loved these get-togethers, as it was a time to catch up with family she would not see that often during the rest of the year. As the family was growing so rapidly, all our children decided to do a Kris Kindle among them and their partners, and they agreed on an amount to spend. Little did they know that would be the last Christmas that they would share this new gift-giving idea with one another. Rachel was so excited that morning when they opened their gifts together, and Kris Kindle is something that they have never done again since Rachel died.

Rachel loved that her two children could meet up with her cousins' children, and the kids were always so excited to see each other. They would all open up their presents from underneath the Christmas tree, and we always had photos taken. A favourite photo of all of ours was one of the third generation of the family – all the babies and toddlers lined up together. The numbers of the little ones were increasing all the time, and the children were changing so much during the year, it was a part of the day that Rachel loved to see. That particular morning, Rachel was catching up with all the news and swapping stories with all the family. Joe was hanging around and not mixing much, which was normal enough for him. At this point, the children had all opened their presents, and there was a bit of festive pandemonium around the house. Rachel had just stepped into the kitchen to talk to me when Joe followed her in and started to upbraid her for not having had us out to their house for a meal recently. The odd thing was that it wasn't just a passing remark, but a long, personal and hurtful attack. I was appalled, as I knew that he wasn't worried about entertaining us – he just used it as an excuse to hurt Rachel. I tried to defuse the situation, coaxing Rachel to stay, but she got so upset that her eyes started to fill with tears and she proceeded to put the children's toys in their bags, got their coats on and hurried them out to the car. Ann tried to persuade her to come back inside and wait for the photos, but Rachel was too shaken and left, saying that they had to go to Joe's mother's and they were running late. She must have felt so disappointed and confused by what had happened, and Joe just showed her no mercy at all about such a small thing.

I was angry that he had ruined her day – her Christmas – and I could not make out for the life of me why he was so cross with her. It was never even an issue with us, not going to Rachel's house for a meal. I always understood how big a deal it would have been for her, as she just was not that great at cooking. I remember her commenting to us on several occasions that she would have us out, but I always assured her that it was not important as she had her hands full with the two babies. Rachel always made up for it in many other ways, and, as any mother knows, all of our children are different and all have their own way of showing their love for us. I wouldn't say that Joe was one bit concerned about us being asked up for a meal – he probably wouldn't even have been there anyway. I know now that he just said it to hurt Rachel, and he certainly succeeded in doing that. It seems now that he just could not bear to see her happy and surrounded by her family who loved her. I never looked for any faults in Joe and I buried any anxiety I felt about instances like these. In my wildest dreams I would never have thought him capable of living the double life he was, and Rachel was probably the same. I wonder now how much she did know, but regardless of what she may have suspected, I'm sure that she loved Joe and did not want to accept her suspicions.

Jim recalled that the year before, in 2002, when he had to have a triple heart bypass, Joe had not come to visit him in hospital or even phoned him to ask how he was feeling. This was strange in many ways, particularly because, in addition to being Jim's son-in-law, he also had a good relationship with our son, Anthony. Anthony and Rachel had always been very close, and Anthony got to know Joe very well through playing softball with them. He would have been a regular presence in Rachel's house in the beginning, and, as he and Joe shared a great interest in films, the two of them would often go to see the latest releases together, and Joe would come to the house regularly enough to collect Anthony to go to the cinema. Even after he was back at home, Jim noticed that, when Joe called over to pick up his brother-in-law to see a film, he would stay outside in the car and ring Anthony from his mobile to come out. He never, ever, once, even asked how Jim was doing since the surgery, nor did he ask after him when he spent time with Anthony. I was very anxious for Jim at the time, as we all were, and I did not even notice Joe's behaviour, but obviously Jim felt hurt by it, though he never discussed it at the time. I remember Rachel was very worried about her dad and was very concerned for him, forever dropping in to see him during his recovery. In hindsight, it was very strange that Joe managed to avoid seeing him entirely during those months.

Paul, Rachel's brother, was married in Rome about three months after that, and all of our family went out there to celebrate with them. When I look back on the photographs, I wonder now how we could not see what was staring us in the face.

On the morning of the wedding, Rachel got up very early, as she was to be the hairstylist for all the ladies in the bridal party. It was quite a lot of work, as she had six women whose hairstyles she had to do: me, Ann, the mother of the bride, Kay, the bridesmaids, Helen and Lynda, and finally the bride, Denise. She did a beautiful job on all of us, and everyone was ready on time except for Rachel

herself – that was just how she was, putting everyone else before herself. I remember her trying to
blowdry her own hair at the very last minute as we
were all heading out the door.

We had a great day full of happy memories –
all of us, that is, except for Joe. He was being his
usual self, not a great mixer, we thought. In the
middle of the celebrations that evening, he went up
to their room at around 9 p.m., leaving Rachel on
her own at the reception. It being her brother's
wedding, Rachel was thoroughly enjoying being
with the family, and was right in the middle of a
sing-song with the rest of the group. I wonder now
how she really felt, being left on her own at a family
wedding without his company. She tried to make
the most of the situation, but she must have felt
very hurt.

Late that night, as the group was winding down,
all of the young people decided to go out and
sample the nightlife in Rome, as they didn't want
the party to end. Rachel decided that she would
stay back and join Joe, as he had gone to bed early.
Ann tried again and again to persuade her, but
reluctantly the group went ahead, while Rachel
stayed back with Jim and me and the remainder of
our group a while longer before going up to Joe
that night. In hindsight, it seemed very unusual to

us that he left her on her own, whereas she didn't want to leave him.

Jim took the wedding party out for a meal the following evening. Declan's wife, Denise, had gotten a recommendation for an Argentinian restaurant a good distance from the hotel where we were staying – a friend of hers had been there on an earlier visit and thought it was great. We were not disappointed. The atmosphere was magic. The restaurant was situated at the end of a series of cobbled streets, the tables were set up outside, and you could hear the sound of the river Tiber near by. It was a very old building, and during the meal the staff laid on a show, with some of them appearing out of upstairs windows, throwing back the shutters and singing as only the Italians can. There were several nationalities among the guests, and we all took it in turns to sing in our own language. The Irish table was called on for an encore, and we all joined in and got into the spirit of things and had a great night. Rachel joined in with the singing, too, and was really enjoying the jokes our friend Myles was telling, as only he could tell them. She always enjoyed our friends' company, and most of them she would have known since she was a child.

I remember it as being a lovely night out, but since Rachel's death, when I look back at the photographs of that dinner, we are amazed that we didn't notice the sullen look on Joe's face and how Rachel did not seem to have the same sparkle in her eyes. I cannot know what Rachel was thinking, but she had to have been more aware of what was going on with Joe than we were. I just wish that she had been able to talk to us, but she was a very proud person and did not want to reveal a negative picture of their relationship.

Though we were slow to pick up on any serious problems evolving between them, there were a few things you just couldn't miss about Joe's behaviour. I rarely saw Joe when I dropped up to their house, as I tended to go during the day, so that I could see the children. Likewise, Rachel would have been calling in to see Jim and me with the children during the day after they spent a few hours in the crèche, which would have been while Joe was at work. But in the months leading up to Rachel's murder, if I arrived at their house and Joe happened to be there, he would avoid being in the same room as me. As I would walk into the kitchen, he would walk into the sitting room, and if I went into the sitting room, he would walk into the kitchen. It was very peculiar. He was never rude and never said anything, he was just cold, and I said as much to Jim. Jim just thought that he wasn't a very good mixer, but then, we knew that already. Now I know that Joe didn't want to enter into any kind of conversation with me, as he was being unfaithful to my daughter and must have been playing it safe.

As strange as I found his behaviour towards me, it was impossible to know from this what he was like when he was alone with Rachel.

Occasionally, though, we got a window into how life was in their home. The summer the year before she died, which was her first summer in Lambay View, Jim and I returned from Mass one Sunday morning to find Rachel waiting in the driveway with the two children. She was in tears and very upset, and they had been there for some time, having arrived just after we left. I had never seen her in such a state before and I wanted her to come in so that I could try and calm her down. She said that she was on her way over to St Anne's Park to meet up with the team for softball practice, and so refused to come in as she didn't want to keep all of the others waiting. She did not say why she was so upset, so I asked her if it was over a row with Joe, but she never really answered me. I never did learn what it was about. What worried me more still was that, the whole time she was there, the two children were sitting in the car without a bother on either on them. Her youngest child was not even two, and her eldest had just turned three a few months earlier, and I thought to myself that if my children had seen me that upset at their age, they would have been hysterical. When she left, I remarked to Jim they must have seen their mother extremely upset before. I wish now that I had insisted on her coming in. Maybe she would have opened up, maybe she would have told me what happened ... but that was Rachel, a proud and private kind of person. I held back then as I had before because, although I always try to be there for my children, I never want to interfere in their lives. I am so sorry that I did not get involved, but I had no idea of the true circumstances of Rachel's life with Joe; now with hindsight, it is possible to see things much more clearly.

Not too long after that incident, the softball team went to Florida. Rachel could not go as she had to stay at home to take care of the children – but Joe went. I just accepted what Rachel told me about it, and it was never discussed. I didn't have a clue that there were any problems in their marriage, as Rachel still continued to speak of Joe in glowing terms. I have no doubt that, whatever was going on with Joe at that time, she was still besotted with him. Rachel had her thirtieth birthday while he was away, and I have since learned that she was very upset because Joe did not even ring to wish her a happy birthday; instead, he sent her a text. I wonder now if she suspected something, because I know that she voiced her disappointment about it to some of her friends. Naturally enough, turning thirty was a milestone for Rachel, and she felt it was somehow unimportant to Joe, seeing as she was on her own.

Rachel, Ann and I had a great girls' day out to celebrate her thirtieth, and we went to town to ensure that she spoiled herself with lots of new treats. As we strolled along Grafton Street through all the high-street women's shops, looking to pick out a few nice things for her in Wallis or A|wear, she strayed into Marks and Spencer and Brown Thomas, ducking in to see if there was anything her family might need, even though it was her birthday. In the end, she did choose some lovely clothes for herself, and we could see her delight, for she had thoroughly enjoyed the day. It is heartbreaking, as little did we realize that it was to be her last birthday.

Shortly after Joe returned from Florida, I was out at Rachel's one morning, and we were up in their bedroom. Rachel wanted to show me the two gorgeous little fancy-dress outfits for the children that Joe had bought in the States for Hallowe'en. One was a dinosaur costume, and it was perfect. The other was a little Peter Pan outfit, which was absolutely gorgeous. When Rachel showed me the two little suits, I asked her what present Joe had brought for her. At this stage, I still had absolutely no idea that there were any serious problems between Joe and Rachel, so I didn't know what to think when Rachel was reluctant to show me what he had bought for her. She told me he had bought her a fancy-dress outfit as well, and, without thinking anything of it, I said I would love to see it. Rachel then took out a witch costume. She was clearly upset about it, and I tried to make her feel better by saying that it had probably cost a lot of money, and that she would look beautiful in it, as she always did no matter what she wore. Rachel replied, 'Where would I get the chance to dress up? It's not something we do. Mam – a witch's outfit?' I knew she was very unhappy about it, and though I was a bit taken aback by Joe's choice of present for his wife, I would never have imagined anything sinister about it, and although dressing up at Hallowe'en was a tradition in our family, it was not something that they did as a family. I think Rachel was hoping that things with Joe would improve, so I didn't press her. Rachel was a very private person, but I wish that I could have been more clued in, and that I could have helped. Although I missed the significance of the witch outfit, Rachel certainly did not, and I now wonder how he could have been so very cruel. I thought that it was particularly horrible of him to ruin this for her, because, like me, Hallowe'en through to Christmas was Rachel's favourite time of the year, and she so enjoyed sharing the excitement of the holidays with the children. As I look back at her last Hallowe'en and Christmas, I feel so very sad for her and wish once again I had registered all of the signs and added up what was happening and that I could have done something to help.

Rachel's life revolved around her family. Her husband and her children were her main focus, and she did everything she could to enrich their lives and care for them. She was a great shopper when it came to spending money on the family, and she made careful choices. Her friends remember her for always looking for the bargains, and she did a great job managing their family budget. Unlike a lot of young women, she would never dream of living beyond their means. I miss her cheery calls when she would ring and say, 'I'm thinking of going to Blanch, are you interested?' I have never made the trip to Blanchardstown shopping centre since she died without feeling her loss. It's only a small thing, of course, but it was Rachel who brought me there the first time I visited it. The same goes for the Pavilions shopping centre in Swords, where I went with Rachel when it first opened. The new part of the motorway had just opened a few months after she moved to The Naul, which made our trips back and forth much easier. I can feel her presence every time I travel that road now, and it feels so real that I often talk to her as I drive along.

I remember that, the Christmas before she was murdered, Rachel and I were shopping in the Pavilions in Swords with the children. We were in Clarks, where Rachel was getting them their shoes for Christmas. The little one, just two at the time, was in the buggy – Rachel wouldn't be alive for her child's third birthday – and was kicking up a fuss because it was taking so long to get the older one's shoes. Rachel liked one pair, as she thought they were more suitable, but her eldest pointed to a pair with dinosaurs on them. I persuaded Rachel to get her choice, telling her that once they were put in the box, the other shoes would be forgotten once everyone got home. I later found out that the child threw a tantrum when they returned, and certainly did remember the other shoes. Rachel returned the next day and bought the second pair secretly, and Santa brought them for Christmas. Rachel was like a big kid herself, getting them their Santa gifts. I can only imagine how those two little children must have felt when they realized that Rachel wasn't around for them any longer.

More than little treats for the children, Rachel had a good eye for shopping for the house. She was forever making improvements to their home after they moved in. She had new windows fitted, and a friend of theirs fitted an electronic garage door for them. All of it made a great difference to the appearance of the house, and she liked making it a better and more attractive home for her family, bit by bit. We had gone out shopping for interior doors for the rest of the house, and eventually she had those changed as well. One of the things that Rachel loved best about living out there was pottering about the garden, and she often liked to pick up a few plants while we were out shopping. One day she bought some young apple trees and had just planted them a few days before I saw them. I felt that they were a bit too near the front fence, and planted a bit too close to each other, but I remember her saying to me, 'I am not going to replant them, sure they'll be all right,' and she was right, they did grow. In time, they blossomed and bore fruit, but, sadly, she isn't there to see them grow. I always feel that a part of her is there in that garden.

Just as the trees were settling and developing new roots, so were her children. The eldest started in a local crèche when they moved to Baldarragh and was very happy there. Rachel was proud to see her child learn and develop. Soon the youngest was old enough to go and was about to leave the nest for a few hours every day, by which point the eldest was about to start primary school.

As the crèche had a place for Rachel's youngest, she started to put a huge effort into finding a 'big school' for her eldest child. She went to visit a nearby primary school and fell in love with it. I recall her saying to me, 'Mam, it's just like a real country school with a real country feeling about it.' She enjoyed getting everything ready: school uniform, gym clothes and all that would be needed. She had been so looking forward to the day her first child would be going to school. I still have an envelope that she had written her child's name on with the milk money for school, the same handwriting that is on another envelope, holding one of the children's curls of hair. She had two boxes at home that she called their treasure chests, and she had put things in them from time to time from when they were infants. She intended to continue right through until it was time for them to leave home, and then she was going to give each of them their own box. She was so looking forward to seeing them grow up. She was so proud of her eldest the first day at primary school, but, God love her, she would only bundle her child out the door in that uniform for four short weeks of 'big school' before she met her brutal and tragic end. Those two little children were her whole life.

We are so glad that Rachel had so many supportive and loyal friends, who were all a huge part of her life. I look back on memories of barbecues and get-togethers she enjoyed with her friends from softball, Helen and Pat, over at their house. Helen used to invite Anthony as well, and Rachel would bring him along and she always looked forward to these events. It used to remind me of our own circle of friends, and I was glad that she also had that in her life, and I like to think that her friends like Jackie, Celine, Paula and all of the girls she spent time with must have given her back some of her sense of worth that was being so insidiously undermined by Joe. Not only did they play a major part in her life, they were instrumental in our fight for justice after she died.

As I said, I worried for Rachel when she moved out to The Naul, because it was so isolated, so I was glad that, when Rachel moved house, she made some new close friends, like Sarah, Michelle, Fidelma and many more. During those days, she must have needed all the warmth and friendship she could get. On reflection, it must have been a very hard and confusing time for her, and I always wondered why she never confided in anyone. I suppose that she was being told such terrible things about herself so often that maybe she began to believe it herself.

The worst part is that Rachel was so genuine and such a kind person herself, she would have had difficulty accepting that Joe was being purposely cruel – and she would never have seen him as being at fault. It breaks my heart that she was just trying to do and be her best for a man she could never please. I think she felt that, whatever was wrong, she would just work harder to make it right. For Rachel, it was simple: she loved Joe uncondition-ally. But the harsh reality was just as simple, and I marvel that we were in such denial that we just could not see what was going on.

One example is how Rachel and Joe felt about Christmas, which she took as just a difference of personalities. While Rachel loved everything about Christmas, she told me on many occasions that Joe had little or no interest in Christmas decorations. I guess you might say that I am a bit over the top when it comes to Christmas, and one of the best parts for me is adding to our decorations each year. The house always looks so warm and festive. Rachel would have been the same, particularly once she had her own house, and even though Joe didn't feel the same, I think he could have made more of an effort for her sake. I went out to the house in Baldarragh just before Christmas 2003 and she had put up the Christmas tree – alone – a few days before that. The children were tumbling around the room, excitedly showing me the tree, jumping up and down and pulling at it. I was surprised to see that it was very unsteady in its stand, and the few decorations that she had put on it looked sparse, and a few of them were broken. I sensed that her spirit was not in it that year, and, though she was doing her best, she did not have the same enthusiasm as she normally would, and I put it down to the upheaval of the house move and all the work she was involved in. It was to be the first and only Christmas she would spend in that house before she died, and I know now that it was not a happy one, and I now know the reasons why.

When I reflect and think about his behaviour in our house on that Christmas morning in 2003 and wonder if he let his mask slip in front of us that day, what in God's name was he putting Rachel through behind closed doors? I feel so angry now at what Rachel had to suffer and more poignantly suffer alone. We will never really know what Rachel went through at Joe's hands; we can only speculate from what we discovered through the evidence of the trial of his true devious character.

5. The Fourth of October 2004

Monday 4 October 2004 a nightmare began from which I have never really woken up. I had no indication that it would be the day that would change our lives for ever as I got dressed that morning.

I am aware that the sequence of my memories may differ from the actual events as they happened, but I have done my best to recall the events of that awful day as honestly as I can. It was a horrific trauma, and it is difficult at times to piece together what happened with a clear mind.

It was a beautiful, crisp, sunny autumn day, very dry and mild for the time of the year. Jim, Declan, Paul and Anthony were working at home that day, and it was unusual for all of them to be there at the same time, so Jim decided to make the most of it to finish painting the outside of the house together while the weather was so good. Aside from the painting, nothing else was in any way out of the ordinary that day. I decided to do a mixed grill for lunch, and the lads were sitting around the kitchen table eating and chatting among themselves. I was standing at the cooker frying the last egg for myself before I sat down to join them. It's funny, but I still remember every single detail of the lunch hour that would change my life for ever.

The phone rang, and, as Anthony was sitting nearest to it, he picked it up. I was only half-listening, as I assumed it was just a call from a customer of Jim's. Anthony was still on the phone when he asked me if I'd heard from Rachel at all that morning. I said, 'No,' and when Anthony hung up, he said it was Joe, wondering if Rachel was here or if I'd been in contact with her during the morning.

'Why does Joe not know where Rachel is?' I asked Anthony, as it seemed so odd that he wouldn't. It was only then that Anthony told me that the crèche had contacted Joe to say that Rachel had not collected their youngest. Immediately, I felt very uneasy. I knew without a doubt that something was wrong if Rachel failed to collect either of the children without letting someone know. What's more, it was unusual for Joe to ring the house at this point, because he had been cutting himself off from us for months beforehand – he would have contacted Rachel directly on her mobile phone. I knew in my heart that something had happened, as it just did not feel right. If for any reason Rachel was delayed, she definitely would have got in touch with myself, a neighbour or any one of her friends to pick up the children. I got Anthony to ring Joe back immediately, and Joe said he was on his way out to pick up the children. I got on to the phone and said I would go to the house. I voiced my fears to Joe, telling him I was very worried that something might have happened to Rachel to prevent her from picking up their youngest child. Joe explained that he had been trying to contact Rachel all morning without success and that he was very worried as well. He said he would collect the children and see me out at the house.

When I finished talking to Joe, Jim wanted to know if Joe had contacted Sarah, Rachel's friend, who lived quite near them in The Naul. Jim was wondering if Joe had got someone to check the house in case Rachel had fallen off a ladder or was perhaps lying injured in the garden, as she did all the work in the garden and the DIY around the house herself. Anthony rang Joe back again, and Joe said he did not have any of his neighbours' phone numbers, that Rachel had all of that kind of thing. Jim asked for the crèche phone number as he knew that Helen at the crèche would probably have Sarah's phone number, as she knew Sarah. Joe sent a text back to Anthony with the number, and Jim contacted Helen and got Sarah's phone number and rang her.

At this stage, I was already half-way up the motor-way. The traffic was moving along well that lunchtime, and I was making very good time going out. The sun was shining, it was a beautiful day, and I tried to remain positive as I got nearer to the slip road for the turn-off. I remember thinking that Rachel must have been in a car accident. 'Dear God,' I prayed, 'do not let her be badly injured.' I started wondering why, if she had been in a car accident, someone hadn't used her phone to contact us, as she never went anywhere without her mobile. I tried not to panic as I got nearer the house and was somewhat relieved to see Rachel's Renault Scenic in the driveway as I pulled in. I drove right up and parked behind Rachel's car.

As I was about to get out of the car, I noticed the two dogs, Jordan and Clio, to the right, huddling together by the hedge. Normally, the dogs would run up to me as soon as I got out of the car, and in that split second I remember thinking that I was going to have a job trying to keep the pair of them out when I opened the patio door into the kitchen, as they always used to get in between your feet and wiggle in the door before you. I always managed to let them in, and Rachel would just laugh. But that day, although the biggest dog, Jordan, came over as I got out of the car, he just stood beside the car wagging his tail. Clio joined him slowly, but it only dawned on me later that they made no attempt to follow me on to the decking and into the house, even though the patio door was wide open. Those two dogs did not want to go in at all. Whatever they saw and heard that morning, they would not set foot in that house. I only wish I could block out everything that happened once I stepped through the door that day.

As soon as I'd seen the door wide open, I immediately felt very uneasy. I crossed the decking and stepped into the kitchen. Something was wrong: it felt different, and although that feeling had registered in my mind, I could not say why until I was giving my first statement to the police. It was then that I could understand and put it into words.

It was the kitchen curtains – they were drawn that morning, and it was unusually dark in the house. I knew that Rachel would not have given the children their breakfast with the curtains drawn like that, nor had I ever known her to draw the curtains during the daytime – I was certain of it. The kitchen table was at an odd angle to the rest of the room and had small piles of clothes sorted and folded on it. The strangest thing was that the tap was running at full blast into the sink, and the contents of some of the kitchen drawers were on the floor. As soon as I saw the things on the floor, I thought it looked staged, not like the random mess a burglar would leave. I looked into the utility room off the kitchen and, though I could not swear to it now, I think I saw a red or green light on the washing machine, as if a wash had just finished, but as far as I know, the washing machine was turned off when the police arrived. I began to call out Rachel's name as I went deeper into the house. I walked into the lounge and saw videos and other things scattered on the floor by the corner unit. The doors to the corner unit were wide open, and I had never seen them like that before. I walked across the length of the room and stood looking down at the things scattered about the floor.

My sense of unease was growing rapidly by this stage, as I was very frightened. I continued back across the room into the hall again, calling to Rachel as I went. All the time, I had a very weird, hollow sensation that I can best describe now as a gut feeling that something was very wrong. I continued on up the hall and looked into the bathroom on the right. At this stage, I was just going quickly from room to room, looking for her. I couldn't see any sign of her when I looked into the bathroom and behind the door and continued on into the children's room next door on the right. Still no sign of her, and everything seemed to look all right in there. I walked out of the children's room and across the corridor to Rachel and Joe's room directly opposite. Just before I put my foot forward to step into the room, I looked down, and part of me died right there and then. It could have been an abattoir, there was so much blood splattered everywhere. When I looked around, I saw blood on the walls, the ceilings, the doors out into the hall and even on the hall ceiling and across the hall in the bathroom – I still do not know how I could have missed it when I first looked into the bathroom. It was then that I looked down and saw my poor child. Rachel was lying in such a horrific state that I will not attempt to describe the scene that I discovered there, but the image of it will haunt me until my dying day. Many times since, when I was at my lowest, I wished that I had died as well that terrible day.

*

Right from the start Rachel captured our hearts. Jim says he will always remember her as the little girl out of the fairy-tale books, like Heidi or Alice in Wonderland. She always did look so beautiful in her pretty little dresses with her hair shining like silk, silver white in the sun, and her skin as brown as a nut.

The picture on the right shows her aged about two and a half in 1976.

Below: Rachel photographed in 1977, with her brothers Paul (*left*) and Declan (*right*).

The top picture shows us on a family holiday in Spain in the summer of 1977 with Rachel, Paul and Declan.

Left: Rachel ready to set off for her first day of school in September 1978.

Below: A school portrait taken in February 1979.

I will never forget
how excited Rachel
was on the day
of her First Holy
Communion in
May 1980.

Left: Declan, Ann,
Rachel and Paul
in 1979.

When Rachel was in her early teens we went to live in Australia for a year. The picture above shows us in California during our extended trip back to Dublin. By now our family was complete: Declan, Ann, Rachel, Paul and our youngest child, Anthony, at the front.

Rachel (13) in Bangkok on the way to Australia.

Rachel (14) in Hawaii on the way home from Australia.

Once Rachel started to date Joe O'Reilly her heart was his forever. By the time this picture was taken, when she was about twenty, they had been going out for a few years.

Rachel and I before her debs in September 1990.

A picture from Rachel's Canadian holiday with Joe, 1993.

Rachel's wedding day in April 1997. Like a lot of brides-to-be, the planning of the wedding seemed to take over her life, and she enjoyed every minute of it. It was a joy to see her so excited about their big day.

The picture above is of our family – Declan and Paul on either side of the bridal couple, Ann to Jim's left and Anthony beside me.

Left: Rachel's new in-laws, the O'Reillys, showing Joe's sister Anne, mother Anne and brother Derek.

I had often heard it said that a girl made a 'radiant bride', and indeed I had seen many brides in my time, but never one as radiant and beautiful as Rachel. It was a bright day, quite mild for April, and I will always hold dear the memory of how she looked that day.

Here are Jim and Rachel dancing at the wedding reception. He was so proud of Rachel on her special day. The picture below right shows the happy couple at Dublin Airport before setting off on their Kenyan honeymoon.

Joe appeared to be fairly normal to us, but we were to learn how well he could mask his true personality. Here he is in a jokey mood at our house on Christmas Day 1999. It was a wonderful time when our family was expanding. Rachel was six months pregnant and the picture also includes Declan's wife, Denise.

Joe with Jim and Anthony on Christmas Day 1999. Anthony looked up to Joe so much. They shared an interest in films, and spent a good amount of time together over the years, so he was later devastated when he learned what Joe had done to his sister and her children.

As soon as I found Rachel, I knew she was dead, and it was clear that she had been murdered. I knelt down beside her and kept saying her name over and over again, as if in some way if I called her enough she could hear me, though I knew in my heart that she could not. As I knelt beside her, all I wanted to do was to help her, but all I could do was to stroke her arms and to keep on talking to her. It felt like I was there for hours, and I have never felt so lonely, so utterly desolate as I did in that house on that day. It was unbearable to know that someone had done something so unimaginably brutal to our precious child, and I was overwhelmed by how alone she must have felt when she knew she was going to die. That feeling will stay with me for ever.

I do not know how long I stayed kneeling down beside Rachel and talking to her. I remember I was afraid to touch her head in case I would hurt her, although I knew she was dead, but I was very aware that I must not touch anything. Time seemed to be standing still. I finally got up off my knees and ran back up to the kitchen table, where I had left my mobile phone. I lifted my phone and tried to ring Jim or home, but I could not physically manage to coordinate my head and my hands – I think I just kept screaming. I went back down to Rachel and knelt beside her and started talking to her again. I remember feeling like there was nobody else in the world apart from the two of us, I felt so lonely and helpless. Again, I realized that I had to contact somebody for help, and I got up and went back to the kitchen. As I entered the kitchen the second time, I spotted Rachel's new landline phone on the side of her overhead unit. I lifted the phone and tried dialling several different times but I was in such a state I could not even dial 999. I kept on trying and, by some fluke, I got through to an actual number – but it wasn't the emergency services that I'd dialled. A man answered the phone and I begged him again and again to send an ambulance for my daughter. I must have been completely incoherent and I think the poor man must have thought that I was some madwoman on the phone. He asked me who I was, and all I could say was that I thought my daughter was dead. I can't remember most of what he or I said, but I do remember him asking me for the address, which thankfully I was able to give him. I never found out who that man was and I still do not know if he was the first to alert the police, but I'm very grateful to him regardless.

I had just hung up the phone and was on my way back down to Rachel again when Rachel's friend Sarah arrived. She told me later she could hear my screams from the road. When she came in, she went straight in to Rachel, and got straight on the phone to 999. As she was talking, my mobile rang. It was my son Declan, ringing from home to find out whether Rachel had turned up yet. Our Declan is a very quiet, gentle person, and when he asked if Rachel had arrived home, he was shocked by my answer. He kept saying, 'She can't be,' and 'How do you know?' Then Jim took the phone from him, as I guess he knew from Declan's reaction that something terrible had happened. I never want to have to tell my loved ones news like that again as long as I live. From that point in time, everything seemed to happen very quickly – the horrible spell was broken as help started to come. Rachel and I were no longer alone, and on one level I was relieved, thinking, 'At least now we have some help. Thank God, now someone will know what to do.' I'll never understand how our minds can register so many things on so many levels in the middle of a crisis, but I guess that I was thinking that, once help came, everything was going to be all right. God help me, it was just as well I didn't know then what lay ahead of us.

After Sarah arrived, I couldn't say how long it was until Joe arrived. In one way, some scenes from that day are frozen in my mind like stills from a film, while other memories seemed to flash through my head as if on fast-forward. I remember hearing a car stop outside, and my instant reaction was that Joe was about to walk into the house with the children, and I knew I could not let this happen. I ran out of the kitchen on to the decking and, as I ran on to the driveway, I could see two cars outside the gate. One car was in front of Joe's — I later learned it belonged to a friend of Rachel's, Michelle — and Joe's Fiat Marea was parked outside the gate in front of the driveway on the road. Although I had never met Michelle before Rachel died, I really felt as if I knew her already. She had become another good friend of Rachel's, and I was very familiar with her name, and stories about her little boy, Dillon. Joe had picked one child up from their crèche — but Rachel and Michelle had a rota between them for picking up the children (and I'm quite sure that Joe would have been aware of this); in the end Michelle had already collected the eldest before Joe arrived at the school. So Joe had the youngest with him, and Michelle had the eldest, when they got to the house, and they arrived at the same time. The scene moved before my eyes as if in slow motion. I can still see Joe in my mind's eye as he stood there on the far side of the car, his face smiling over at me. I clearly remember thinking to myself, 'How am I going to tell him?' It seemed unthinkable to tell him the horrific news, to try to prepare him for what he was about to find out. When I realized later that Joe already knew what I had found when I entered the house that day, I feel sick when I recall him smiling at me. That image, along with so many others, will never leave me.

My main concern at that moment was that Joe would walk into the house with the children. I remember saying to him as fast as I could that I thought Rachel was dead. Looking back, I was avoiding the very word 'murder', although I knew that was what had happened. I was devastated for him, this young man with two children little more than babies, having to face what would tear life as they knew it apart. I said a few quick words to Michelle, and she turned to take them by the hand back to her car. God only knows exactly what I said to her, but I was horrified to hear the oldest one ask, 'Who's dead?' I said something about nobody being dead and gave thanks for young innocence as the children happily went off with Michelle, without a clue that everything had changed in the few hours since their mother's kiss goodbye that morning.

I ran back into the house through the patio door

in the kitchen just behind Joe and I remember telling him that Rachel was down in the bedroom. I felt as if my heart would break for him – I could hardly breathe. The first thing he did was to place two fingers on Rachel's neck to check if there was a pulse. Obviously, there was not, and as he had first aid training, he would have known that. It is only now I realize that, even from the very first moment I saw Joe there, I was confused by his reactions that day. I waited for him to take Rachel in his arms, to cry, to shout out – it was clear that she was dead and had died in horrific, violent circumstances. I would have expected him to lift her and to hold her, particularly as it was not as if he was afraid he would contaminate any evidence. When he tried and failed to get a pulse, he then proceeded to pull boxes of things and objects from around Rachel's head and to fling them into the children's room directly behind him on the other side of the corridor. I was very aware that Joe was contaminating evidence, whether he was aware of it or not. Instinct told me not to touch anything, and I guess he knew he shouldn't either, but at the time I thought it was just grief that made him act this way. I remember feeling quite sick and wanting to tell him not to do that, I was silently screaming for him to stop, but I just stood there in shock and let him.

He didn't actually move Rachel's head, just the stuff that surrounded her, so really he made quite a show of doing nothing. I thought that, as he had trained in first aid, he would have been able to help her, but he never even tried. I said to him that maybe there was some hope, maybe there might just be some tiny spark of life left in Rachel, but I knew it wasn't true. I guess I was trying to give him some hope to cling on to, and he went along with it, knowing full well that he had made one hundred per cent certain not to leave Rachel there alive.

Joe never at any stage tried to lift Rachel or, as he later said, to give her CPR. I was next to him the whole time, and he never touched her beyond placing his two fingers on her neck and pulling things out from around her head. His words to her that morning shocked me to the core. When he bent over the horrifically battered and lifeless body of his beautiful wife, he said, 'Jesus, Rachel – what have you done?' I remember thinking, 'What does he mean "What has she done?" Rachel has been murdered.' He never uttered a single word of love to her.

What I witnessed in that room just did not seem normal to me. Joe was not reacting to the bloody scene of his wife's brutal murder in the way I would have expected at all. Shock, and later, grief, show themselves in many ways, but no loving husband could have taken in the scene that day without some outpouring of anguish. I would discover much later the awful truth of what he did mean by his question to Rachel. In his mind, Rachel had done this to herself, and she was to blame for everything. That's just the way he sees it.

Rachel's best friend, Jackie, was the next to arrive, and, after we told her what we knew, Jackie made her way down to the bedroom to Rachel. I do not remember what Jackie said when she arrived, just her shock and disbelief on being told that she was dead. Somehow, I was expecting Joe to accompany Jackie down to Rachel, bearing in mind that Jackie is a neuro-surgical nurse and she was so close to Rachel, I would have thought that he would want to be with her – but to my surprise he followed me as I made my way into the lounge. I was so agitated at the whole scene that I could not sit down, so I stood there beside the coffee table not knowing what to do or what to say to Joe to comfort him. All of a sudden, he walked over to the coffee table and he picked up a scrunched-up plastic bag and he held it out towards me. 'She got these in Marks and Spencer yesterday and sat there eating them last night as she watched television,' he said to me as he indicated the crumbs left in the bag. Rachel had bought cakes in Marks and Spencer the previous day. It was something that she would often do when she shopped there as she loved their cakes. To think that, when he saw her there eating them that night, he knew it would be the last time she would ever do that is a horrible thought that will never leave me. He said it in such a matter-of-fact way that, even then in my distress, it didn't seem quite right. When I started to picture Rachel sitting there just the night before, I felt so upset I had to get out of the room.

I went back down the hall to where Jackie was still with Rachel, and Joe followed me. Jackie had been trying to move her when we got there, and Joe put his hands on Rachel as if to help, but Jackie knew well that, at this stage, there was nothing she could do. Jackie's face was white with shock as she said to Joe, 'It's no use – Rachel is gone. What the hell happened?', or words to that effect. That was the only time Joe touched Rachel other than when he tried to find her pulse. I cannot remember the exact words that passed between them, but Jackie was very obviously in shock. She gave Joe a hug to comfort him before going back to the kitchen to wash her hands, as they were covered in blood.

The ambulance came next, and soon after they

arrived we were asked to leave the bedroom and go to the kitchen or the lounge so that they could have some space to work. Within a few minutes, Jim and our son Paul arrived. They were in an awful state, Jim in particular. I asked them would they like to go down to be with Rachel, and they both did. I knew that they would want to see her, regardless of how she looked, as any loved one would, no matter what the conditions were. Before we got half-way down the hall we were asked to go back. I think it was a young trainee Ban Garda who had accompanied the ambulance when it arrived at the house, and she was trying to preserve the scene of the crime. We returned to the lounge, but Jim felt sick and could not stay in the house, so we went outside on the decking to get some air. He could not stay still, and we walked up the driveway and on to the roadway just outside the gate.

Everything seemed to speed up again. The police came and quickly started to preserve the whole scene, and just then my sons Declan and Anthony arrived. Without thinking, I started to walk up the driveway with them towards the house, and they were both very upset. We had not gone far when one of the detectives told us we could no longer enter past the gates. They proceeded to put police tape across the gates and entrance into the house, when I realized that my car was parked in the driveway behind Rachel's and my jacket, bag and mobile phone were still in the kitchen, all on the other side of the tape. I was then told that I would not be able to get my car or any of my belongings back, as they would now be kept for evidence. Ironically, it was only afterwards that I learned that Joe's car was not taken for evidence that day, as he had not brought it into the driveway – whether this was a conscious decision on his part, we'll never know. Joe had left his car outside the gate, and so he was able to take it home to his mother's house in Dunleer that night.

Out standing on the roadway, our family was all in deep shock. We had no coats on and, although we were not aware of it, it had grown quite cold. Jim was in shock and shivering badly. A very kind paramedic gently suggested that we sit in the ambulance to get warm and he took out a blanket and wrapped it around Jim's shoulders. By the time we got out of the ambulance, Joe's mother had arrived in a taxi, and I gave her a hug. Once the Gardaí had arrived and preserved the house as a crime scene, we were no longer allowed past the gate. We had no option but to return home.

*

My daughter Ann had been out of work on sick leave for the two weeks previous to Rachel's death and had, as it happened, only just returned to work that morning. We were worried that Ann might hear the news from someone else, as one of our lads had already heard a bulletin about a young woman's body having been discovered in The Naul area. We knew we had to see her and break the news to her ourselves, so Paul drove Jim and myself back on to the motorway as we headed back into the city centre. Paul rang Ann and told her he was working just around the corner and would call and give her a lift home. Ann was glad of the offer as she did not have a car of her own then. All the way out to Ann's work in Drumcondra, I was petrified by the thought that she would hear the news before we reached her. When we got there, Paul waited in the car while Jim and I went in. Over the years, I would have dropped in on my own to see Ann in work at various times, but I would have always rung first. How was I going to tell her? She was going to know that something was not right as soon as she saw both her mam and dad arriving in out of the blue. I was overwhelmed by dread as we walked in that day and I kept praying to God for Him to help me. As soon as Ann saw us in her office, her face lit up in surprise and she smiled at us for a split second, but almost instantaneously her face changed. She has since said that she knew something was wrong, that she knew it was bad news. I don't remember what I said to her, but she tells me that I said we thought that Rachel had been murdered. Having to tell her was one of the hardest things I have had to do in my life, and Jim and I almost had to carry her out to the car.

We drove back to our home in Whitehall. I walked through the hall and into the kitchen, and it felt like a million years had passed since I had left it a few short hours ago. It felt like a completely different world, like I was a stranger in my own home, and indeed, I would soon discover how our life as we had known it no longer existed. Paul and Ann began the awful task of ringing family and friends to let them know the news, but I remember feeling quite strongly that I wanted to tell my own siblings and their families myself. Susan's husband, Kevin, told me afterwards that I had phoned their house, but that my sister Susan was not home and that I asked him to give her the news of Rachel's murder, but I don't have any memory of that call, although I know I must have made it. The first one I remember contacting was my eldest brother, Jimmy. It was May, his wife, who answered the phone. I forced the words out of me, feeling like

I had to do it. The news was so shocking that she could not take it in. I will always remember her shocked words as she said, 'Stop that.' She just refused to accept it, and I couldn't blame her.

It was then that whatever invisible force that had been holding me up so far just crumbled away. I could no longer be strong for Jim, the boys and Ann. I asked May to let the rest of our family know. Once I put the phone down, I just let go. I remember a swarm of people, all of our family and great friends, coming and going that evening, and I never stopped crying. I was stopped in my tracks by vivid flashes of Rachel as I had found her, and reliving the trauma and the shock of it was unbearable. The picture of Rachel lying there in that awful state was burned on my memory, and all I wanted to do was to take her from that cold and lonely house and bring her home. I think that Dr Marie Cassidy, the State Pathologist, was in a different part of the country that afternoon, and could not make it to Rachel's body before it got dark. As a result, Rachel could not be moved until the pathologist had examined it. It would have helped a little if I had realized then that indeed she did have someone there with her. A Garda had stayed at the house throughout that night, and I am forever grateful to him – he will never know how much that knowledge means to me.

I don't know how I survived the rest of that evening. People kept trying to get medical attention for Jim and myself, and, though I did not want to, we eventually agreed and my sister Susan arranged for a doctor to come to the house. He gave Jim and me a shot of something to calm us down. I had never had anything like that before, and, while it did help, it gave me the strangest feeling. I could still feel all the same emotions, but it was as if they were coming from another room, if that makes any sense. Some people describe it as being underwater, but it is a distant, disconnected sensation that didn't put me much at ease. Although I was exhausted, my eyes just refused to close, and I did not sleep much that night. I couldn't close them for fear of what I would see, and it was a fear which would remain with me for a long time. Indeed, sleepless nights are still the norm for us.

The detectives came to our house at a later stage to interview us. We had to hand over the clothes and shoes we were wearing in Rachel's house that day, and each of us had to give hair samples and have our finger- and handprints taken. It all happened through a fog of unreality.

As the week went on, Paul and Denise, who was four months pregnant, stayed in the kitchen with us every night after everyone had left. I was concerned for Denise, as I knew she should be getting a lot more rest than she was, but we appreciated a bit of time to sit together and chat. Paul would not leave until Jim and I were ready to go up to bed, and I remember waving goodbye to them in the early hours of the morning through that week. It was good to have some family time together to talk. Everyone's support during that time was very welcome, as the house felt unnaturally quiet with just ourselves there.

6. Saying Goodbye to Rachel

The next day was a big ordeal, because the police needed me to identify Rachel's body. Rachel was removed from her home in Baldarragh the following day and brought to the morgue in Marino. The day was a blur, and I was dreading the whole process. I went to the morgue with Joe. I hadn't seen Joe since we had left Baldarragh to tell Ann the previous day and was at a loss as how to comfort him. If we were in so much pain, I thought, *what* must it be like for Joe?

'I do not really know what to say to you, Joe,' I said in the car. 'I cannot tell you that I know how you are feeling, only you know that, but I do know that it must be horrific for you. Rachel was our daughter, our child, and I know how we feel, but she was your soul mate, your love and the mother of your two children, and I know your whole world has crumbled. I feel so very sorry for you and I only wish there was something I could do.'

He mumbled something in response, and I couldn't make out any sign of emotion on his face at all. I didn't know what to think, but my gut reaction was that something wasn't right.

When we arrived at the morgue in Marino, I was taken aback by how cold and unwelcoming it was, so much so that I thought we were in the wrong place. It looked like a few prefab buildings in a large car park. 'Where is the morgue?' I thought to myself. Joe, his brother Derek and myself got out of the car and were approached by Tom Gallagher, the Superintendent of Balbriggan Garda Station, accompanied by Detective Peter McCoy. They explained that there was some delay, and we would have to wait outside until we were told we could go in. Both men promised us that as soon as they got the word, they would let us know, so we went back to sit in the car. I will never forget how devastated I felt as I sat there, while Joe and Derek stood outside in the car park, talking. Time seemed to stand still. I was very anxious to be with Rachel, but dreading it, too. I could hear voices in the background; people in the Fire Brigade training centre and others came and went, parking their cars and passing by without even being aware that we were there. I was deeply sad and felt so helpless as I tried to work out how the world was still going about its business while my heart was breaking. Everything in my world had come to a stop, and my pain was so great, it just seemed impossible that it didn't affect everyone else too. 'How can things look so normal?' I thought. 'Do you not know that life should not be normal? Has no one told you the awful news?' It was another bright, mild day, and I just sat staring at the big trees swaying gently in the wind and the birds flying by across the sky, wondering why those birds were flying at all: had they not all heard? I could hear the busy hum of the traffic near by, and I pictured all the people coming and going about their day without the slightest clue of what had happened. Once, of course, we had been the same – most of the world is totally oblivious to the despair of people around them, as it's impossible to know what people right next to you are suffering.

The moment that I was both dreading and praying for came. The two Gardaí came over and told us it was time. We headed into a very cold and sterile-looking prefab and were told that Derek was not allowed in. I walked through a room that was quite small and bare towards what looked like a hospital trolley. It was covered all over in white sheeting, and, as I approached, I could just see that Rachel's face was visible, and her body and head were covered. There are no words for what I was feeling, but it was as if my heart was breaking in my chest, a physical pain I cannot describe. Fortunately, all that I could see was her beautiful face, though her eye and part of her forehead were badly bruised and swollen; it was hard to witness. When I had first found Rachel's body, I could hardly make out if I was looking at the back of her head or the front. Her head was so badly beaten that I couldn't see her face as she lay in a pool of blood. Somehow, to see her face again was a shock. I managed to utter the words 'Yes, this is my daughter Rachel.' Joe stood by my side, but I was too upset to take in his reaction. When we got back outside those two poor men, Superintendent Tom Gallagher and Detective Peter McCoy, stood there patiently with us as I implored them to let me bring Rachel home. They were so gentle and compassionate as they explained that Rachel had to stay there while the forensics work was done on her body. I suggested that they could come to our house and carry out all that had to be done on her there, but of course I was not thinking straight; my only desire was to bring her home. The police would continue to be helpful and extremely kind to us throughout the whole long and difficult ordeal and they never ceased to be understanding, trying in every way they could to make things as easy on us as possible. I have said many times we can never speak highly enough of the Gardaí.

My memories of the next few days are very blurred. The house was packed every day with family, friends and people coming to pay their respects. Joe would arrive each morning at our house almost every day the week before Rachel was buried. One day, he brought a pile of Mass cards which had been given or sent to him and threw them on the kitchen table, saying, 'There's more of them.' We were surprised that most of them had not even been opened and, when we opened the first few, we didn't recognize the names of the people who had sent them, as we would not have known many of Joe's extended family or colleagues. We said as much to him, as we didn't want people's thoughtfulness to go unnoticed, but he had no interest in even looking at them.

At about the same time, it became clear that the media interest in the case was rising. A few days after Rachel died, Susan, my sister, and May, my sister-in-law, were coming into the house when they noticed Joe's brother Derek sitting in his car in our driveway. Apparently, Joe had just come into the house with one of the children, and Derek was sitting in the car to allow the other child to have a little nap after having fallen asleep on the journey down from Dunleer. Looking back on the night Rachel died, I was so upset and the house was so full all evening that it wasn't until everybody had left the house that I realized that neither Joe nor any of his family had been to our house or even tried to contact us since we had left Baldarragh that evening. I remember being concerned for Joe and, though it was quite late, I rang him and told him I felt we should all be together and that I had almost driven out to be with them. He did not say how he felt one way or the other, and I guess that I just put his offhand attitude down to shock.

Another morning early in that first week, Joe came in with two big brown envelopes and left them on the kitchen table. 'Imagine,' he said, 'they're sending these already.' When we opened them, we saw that they were batches of samples from two different companies of *memoriam* cards. It was very unsettling that Joe never showed any interest whatsoever in Rachel's funeral. It wasn't even that he was too emotional to take part, but the opposite – unbelievably, he seemed to be totally unaffected by Rachel's death and behaved in the most distant, disconnected way. It was bewildering, but it didn't go unnoticed by others. One of our friends went home to his wife the first day and said to her, 'Joe did it.' His wife was shocked and told him not to repeat what he had said to anybody, but having observed Joe throughout the day, our friend said that he could not help but notice Joe's demeanour, and, being very conscious of the fact that Rachel had only died the day before, and considering the state that the rest of the family was in, he was certain that Joe had murdered our daughter. 'I know he did it,' he repeated.

Jim began the sad task of arranging Rachel's funeral and he decided to engage the services of Michael Rock in Swords. Jim's family had always found Rock's to be very good and reliable in looking after the funerals of many of his relations. Sadly, he had had all too much experience in this regard, having buried his parents and his sister Lucy – Sister Declan – who had died unexpectedly in Ireland only a year before, having come from Australia for a holiday. As we were making plans, we felt that it was only right to see what Joe would want, so Jim asked him if there was any other undertaker he would prefer, or if there were any particular arrangements he would like to have included, but his answer was always the same: 'No, anything you decide is OK by me.' It was the same when it came to booking the venue for the refreshments after the funeral. We thought that The Regency Hotel was the most convenient place, but before we actually booked it, we asked Joe if he would rather do it somewhere else, but his answer was the same as before – he would leave all of that to us. Soon, the undertaker, Michael Rock, called into our house to discuss the funeral arrangements with Joe. It turned out that Joe did not want to have Rachel's grave registered in his name, which seemed very odd at the time. Michael explained to him that the normal procedure would be to register it in the husband's name if the deceased was his wife, but Joe said that he did not want to do the normal thing and asked him to register it in Jim's name. One of our good friends was present during this conversation and simply could not believe his ears. It soon became quite clear that Joe wanted literally no part of anything to do with Rachel's funeral or the arrangements for it, but we were so distressed, and so much was going on at the time, that we did not even try to process these peculiar developments.

That week leading up to the funeral was surreal: there were so many things going on, and we were all still in a state of shock, trying to get through each day as best we could. There was so much to do, and so many people around, none of us could even think about trying to make sense of the distressing truth that was starting to emerge. I already knew with certainty that Rachel had not been murdered by a burglar, and that the house had been staged to look like that, but I hadn't taken the next step to ask myself or others who would have gone to the trouble to want to give people that impression. My first real inclination that things didn't add up had come in the first few days after the murder, when television reporters came out to our home to interview Joe, Jim and me. I was at a loss as to who would have wanted to carry out such a savage attack on our daughter but was equally clear that, whoever it was, Rachel had known and trusted them, which is exactly what I told the detectives from the very beginning.

It was while one of the television interviews was taking place, when the crime correspondent started to ask Joe about finding Rachel's body, that I began in earnest to question his answers. I tried to make out how he had known some of the information he was giving, including how he could identify particular areas on her head where he had claimed that she had received blows. I had knelt down beside Rachel when I found her and been very close to her for some time – more so than Joe – and I could never have said where on her head she had been hit. Her poor body was in such a state, it would have been impossible to know without medical examination, but Joe seemed to be able to point them out very clearly. He even held up his arms and pointed to various places where he claimed he saw bruising on Rachel's arms. He said that, although he was no expert, in his opinion, the bruises and scrapes were defensive marks, and that Rachel had tried to defend herself. I was still very conscious of how little time Joe had actually spent by Rachel's body, so I was really puzzled as to how he seemed to know so much about the exact points of her injuries. I did not yet suspect him of having murdered Rachel, but I was beginning to realize that things were not as Joe was laying them out to be. I can still see the look in his eyes as he concluded one of these first early interviews by asking Rachel's murderer, 'Why Rachel? Why did you feel you had to take such a very young life? What did she do in your opinion to deserve this? I feel I know you because you had to kill her. Will you do it again? If you will, you need help. I feel you could not leave her alive to identify you. It is only a matter of time before you are caught.' When I look back on a recording of that same interview, it is chilling to know that in addressing Rachel's killer, he is talking to himself. Even without knowing the truth, it was extremely disturbing to see him speak without the slightest trace of emotion about his wife, who he had lost so tragically just a few days before.

During that same interview, Joe talked about how Rachel would not be around to see their youngest's first day at school, how she would miss both children's First Communions and Confirmations and all the other milestones in their young lives. It is beyond belief to have him articulate on camera that he knew exactly what he was doing to his wife and his children when he carried out this horrendous crime. He knew exactly what he was taking from his own children, but it did not seem to affect him in any way.

From the Monday afternoon of that week until the Friday afternoon, we waited for Rachel to be brought home. The house was full, and the doorbell was ringing constantly, with personal callers, the press and the Gardaí all coming by. Rachel's body was not released until the Friday afternoon, five days after her murder. Due to the fact that neither

Jim nor Paul had seen Rachel on the day of the murder, they both felt that they had to see her before the coffin was closed. We contacted the undertaker, who said that regrettably, he did not think it was a good idea. He tried to advise us to remember Rachel as she had been in life, but Jim and Paul were adamant they wanted to see her no matter how she looked. To his credit, Michael Rock arranged for us to go to the funeral parlour in Swords so as we could see Rachel for the last time and to put our letters to her in the coffin before the lid was sealed. All of us, including Rachel, had done the very same when my dad, Rachel's granddad, died suddenly a few years before; each of us wrote what we wished we could have said to him before he died, and we placed our letters in the coffin with him. We all agreed that it had helped us a lot, so I knew what it would mean to be able to write our thoughts down to Rachel, as the circumstances of her death meant that we had been denied the chance to say goodbye. Everyone very much wanted to write the letters, and as it was Rachel's birthday the following week, we also wrote birthday cards, but not all of us were up to going to the funeral home that day. Declan was very distressed, and he decided that he did not want to see his beloved sister as she was now, but that he wanted to keep his memories of the sister he loved and had grown up with. Anthony also felt that he could not look at what had been done to her, it would have affected him too much. We were able to take their letters out for them and give them to Rachel along with our own. Ann was torn apart with grief, but she also wanted to go and see Rachel. Ann's own overwhelming sadness did not stop her from feeling for us – if it had been humanly possible to do so, she would have gladly borne our grief for us.

It was a rush that evening to get our letters and cards finished, as we were trying to reach Swords early enough so that the undertaker would not get caught up in the peak traffic when he left Swords to return to our home in Whitehall with the hearse. Our friend Vinny drove Jim, Ann and me out in his car, and Rachel's friend Jackie and Joe decided to come along, and they travelled with Paul and Denise. It was a very distressing moment for each of us as we all said our goodbyes to Rachel, kissed her and put our letters and cards in with her. Joe had brought his letter to Rachel, and two plastic toys that he said were from the children, and he placed them alongside her as well. When everyone had finished, Joe was standing there looking in at Rachel, and I said, 'Joe, we will go and leave you to say your goodbyes alone,' as I felt it must have been hard on him with all of us being present. In hindsight, though, he displayed no emotion whatsoever that day, and it didn't seem to make any difference to him. Just a moment after we stepped out, our friend Vinny was shocked to hear Joe say to the undertaker, 'You can put the lid on that now.' Even his choice of words still rattles me, but it was not to be the last shocking thing to come out of Joe before we headed home. The nightmare was beginning to go from bad to worse.

Rachel's presence was strongest during that week. I think she stayed with me until after the funeral and the initial waves of shock had passed. I am convinced that she was nearest during the nighttime, as I wasn't sleeping well at all. One night, I must have dropped off with pure exhaustion, and I had a very vivid dream. My friend Val and I were walking along a narrow road in Italy or Spain or somewhere like that. It was a beautiful sunny day, and I was conscious of the warmth of the sun as we chatted and made our way along the road. After a considerable time, we reached the end of the road, and I realized that it had become quite dark all of a sudden, as if it was twilight. Val indicated to me that she was going to turn right, and I turned left in the opposite direction towards what appeared to be a small town with quaint shops lining the streets. At this stage, I appeared to be pushing a small shopping trolley as I went from shop to shop. When I had finished my shopping, I made my way back up to where Val and I had parted, as we had agreed to meet when we were finished. As I approached the spot, I could see Val coming towards me, smiling. We both turned back on to the long road that we had arrived by, and, as we were making our way back, I saw that the sun was shining again. We both chatted to each other about what we had bought in the little town. 'I must show you what I got,' Val said as she unwrapped a package of what looked like paintings without their frames. 'Pictures are one of my favourite things,' I said to Val as I got a closer look at them. 'I don't know why I didn't go to your side of the town,' I said, disappointed. Val explained that she had come across a little shop that sold many different artists' work, and she held out a bundle of about six canvas pictures with no backing or frames on them. As I looked through them, I was really sorry I had not visited the shop myself. They were scenes with Mexican-looking backgrounds with beautiful colours in various shades of cream, terracotta and apricot, and when I got to the last one, I remember thinking how beautiful this particular one was. I thought how I would have loved to have one just like it. I recall Val offering to walk back to the town with me so as I could get some myself but I felt we had walked too far and it was now too hot under the glare of the sun to consider making the journey back. I still remember that picture as if I had actually held it in my hand. I was looking intently at it in my dream and thinking how beautiful it was when I noticed that the terracotta colour was a robe and, on looking closer, I saw the figure of Christ carrying the Cross. I can still see the Crown of Thorns pushed down on his head. I was shocked and thought to myself, 'Sure, I could not frame and display this, it's a scene from the crucifixion.' I wrapped the pictures up again and handed them back to Val, and we continued our journey down the road.

The next morning, as Jim and I were having our breakfast, I told him about the dream and how real it had been. As I got to the part of the story with the figure of Christ, I stopped and said, 'That's my cross that I have to bear.' That was before I had found out the true horror of what happened. I often think of that dream, and how I had needed to look closer to see the true picture. I wonder if it was another sign of what was to come and the shocking truth we were yet to discover.

*

It was terrible as parents to witness the raw grief around us – both in each other and in our children – and to know that there was nothing in this world we could do to alleviate it. It was something we, each one of us, had to bear, and, as I look back, I marvel at the strength we were given. We needed so much to just be able to get through each day. I love my children very much, I cannot put into words the love and immense gratitude we feel towards them, especially since the death of their sister.

In the midst of our grieving, it was a great help and support to us to have so many neighbours, friends of ours and of Rachel's, and all of our families around us. The house was full for days, and it played a big part in helping us to get through that terrible ordeal. My sister Susan stayed in the kitchen, looking after everyone, and I did not have to worry about people having to get tea, coffee or refreshments, Susan saw to all of that and organized the meals. She even brought cooked meals over, some of which her friends had provided. It was a very odd time on a practical level for us, too, as usually I am very aware of regular meal times and make sure there are proper dinners on the table, as Jim is a diabetic and his diet is essential for his good health. Though I didn't pay much attention to his needs in the week that followed

Rachel's murder, even in my distress, I remembered to make sure that Joe and his brother Derek had their meals and were looked after whenever they were there. Derek was in the house with Joe a lot during that first week; at that time we had no idea what had been going on in Rachel's life, in her home. I had never looked for any negative aspects of any area of Rachel's life, and as the truth came out during the trial, as her mother, I was devastated. It seemed so ironic, because my sister Susan had always heard me say how supportive I felt Joe's mother was to Rachel, and when they met that week, Susan thanked her for being so.

For the two years before Rachel died, her personality was not as bubbly or carefree as before. What I had never known, but was to soon find out, was the cause of Rachel's insecurity. We now know from the evidence produced at the trial that Rachel was being told relentlessly of her lack of mothering instincts: her parenting was constantly criticized and every aspect of her life with the children was under continuous scrutiny. How she was able to function as well as she did given her true circumstances that were brought to light after her death is testimony to her great spirit. If I achieve one thing out of this whole traumatic affair, it will be to show the people who believed Joe O'Reilly's cruel picture of Rachel what a loving a mother she truly was.

Each night after the visitors were gone and it was just family, just before we went to bed, Jim and I would go in to where Rachel was lying in her coffin. The coffin was, of course, closed due to the injuries she had suffered, but we knew what our child looked like and we were so grateful to have her back here with us, even if it was just for three days. We would sit down together beside her and we would talk to her and say a few prayers before we headed upstairs to bed. I do not think we would have been able to bear it if she had not come home, as we found it such a tremendous help, but it was also heartbreaking to have to let her go. The last night she was to spend at home, which was her thirty-first birthday, was the hardest. Paul was inconsolable, and I had tried in vain to comfort him by saying that she would always be with us. I will always feel his pain and distress as he said, 'No, it will never be the same again; she won't be here any more. She is leaving tomorrow for good.' The reality of what he was saying hit home. How were we going to survive the next few days, let alone the rest of our lives?

My friend Val and I used to walk around the

block during that first week just to get a breath of fresh air – it was probably part of the inspiration for my dream, as the mind works in strange ways in times of stress. Though I was not conscious of the doubts that were starting to creep into my mind at that time, Val has since reminded me that I asked her to keep praying, that I felt there were dark days ahead. I had not spoken of my feelings to any-body else as I guess I was trying to keep as positive as I could. The possibility that it was Joe who had killed Rachel was the worst conceivable case for us. It was bad enough that the children had lost their mother in such tragic circumstances, but that it was at the hands of the father they loved was just too much to bear thinking about.

Preparing for the funeral of a murder victim is completely different to that of a loved one who has had a peaceful death. Everything, including the small, upsetting details, is more difficult, some for very practical, basic reasons. As Rachel's house was still sealed off as a crime scene, we could not choose something for her to wear from her own belongings, which was hard enough. Ann and Paul's wife, Denise, had to go into town to buy some clothes for Rachel to be buried in. Rachel would have loved them. It was probably one of the saddest things that hit me that day as I realized that she would always be young to us. What was worse was that it was her birthday, and by rights she should have been out shopping with Ann and Denise, like Ann and I had done the year before with Rachel for her thirtieth birthday.

On the day of Rachel's funeral it was another beautiful, dry, sunny morning on 11 October 2004. The O'Reillys arrived from Dunleer before we left for the church. When we got there, the sheer size of the crowd that had turned up to pay their respects was overwhelming. We had to gather whatever strength we had left to get us through the funeral. Our family sat up in the front of the church next to the altar, and I was worried that I wouldn't be able to hold it together, that Jim and I might not get through it with dignity for Rachel. Joe's mother was sitting in the seat beside us, and Jim took her hand to support her. The Mass itself was very hard, as each one of us recognized that Rachel was now on her final journey. Never again could she be part of our life, and that was something we did not know how we could cope with. It was a beautiful Mass in a very packed church. Shay from the local shop where Rachel once worked said that he had never seen such a crowd at a funeral since Luke

Kelly from The Dubliners was buried, many years before.

A lot of things seemed to go over my head during the funeral, but I was very aware of Joe getting up to address the congregation with the oration that he and his brother Derek had prepared. In a very calm and composed voice, he spoke of Rachel's life. The absence of any words of love in relation to his life with Rachel was glaringly obvious to me. I waited to hear of his love for her, willing him to utter his devastation at her loss, praying that he'd spell out how much he was going to miss her. I wanted so much to hear those words that would have relieved the growing unease at the back of my mind. It was not to be. Instead, Joe spoke about all she had achieved in her short life; in his opinion, she had done it all, achieved all the goals she had set herself, and, in his opinion, she had not missed out on anything. He did thank her for her love and for making him laugh – 'Mission accomplished,' he said, 'Well done.' I thought of all the plans she had for her future, the dreams she spoke about for her two children, how very hard she had worked to get the things she did achieve and could no longer get any pleasure from. 'See you on the other side. We all thank you – bye for now,' he said.

Rachel was robbed of everything that lay ahead

of her, everything she had ever wanted. She was ripped from her two babies and denied the pleasure of being by their side as they navigated their way through life. She would have been their loving and helpful guide, and theirs would have been such a different life to what they were left, but Joe feels she had it all. Before he stepped down, he said that he had something to say to the person responsible for Rachel's death. In that same measured, emotionless tone, he declared: 'Unlike you, she is at peace. Unlike you, she is sleeping. She forgives you, and I hope she gives me the strength to one day forgive you.' I felt like I had the wind knocked out of me. How could he say that Rachel forgives the person who dealt her such a brutal and painful death? How could he say that she would forgive the beast that left her two babies traumatized and without the presence and guidance of their loving mother? How could he possibly claim to know what Rachel would tell us – if only she could. It could have all been so different, but there was sadly never an option for her. If Joe had been honest with Rachel and told her he had found someone else, they could have taken the normal route of getting a divorce. I know that Rachel would have been heartbroken, but I have no doubt that she would have worked it out with him. She would have made a very good life for herself and the two children – she was so capable – and she certainly would have wanted the kids to have their father in their life. Why couldn't he have given her a chance?

The card on the flowers Joe got for his wife's funeral said it all: 'See you later, Joe.' Not another word, just that stark message amid the outpouring of compassion on cards, some from total strangers who just wanted to give her flowers in support. By contrast, Joe's message did not even refer to his wife by name, and, as always, love was never mentioned.

7. 'Mam, he did it'

Once the funeral was over, Joe was told by the police that he could go back to the house in Baldarragh the following day, Tuesday 12 October. Joe claimed that this was so that he could 'identify any items missing from the house'. While he was there, the police returned the keys of the house to him, and he told Jim and me later that day that he had experienced a great sense of peace and a feeling of calmness when he returned to Lambay View. He told us that he had felt Rachel very near to him in the house. He said that he intended to go back the next day and asked us if we would like to go also. It was the last place I ever wanted to set foot in again, but Jim said, if it had that effect on Joe, then maybe it would be good for us, so reluctantly, I agreed to go.

Jim travelled out to the house in Joe's car, and, as they were driving out, Joe's mobile phone rang. When he hung up, he looked at Jim and said, 'It has started already. That was a colleague of mine ringing to tell me the rumours have started about me having an affair.' Jim tried to reassure him by telling him we would never believe anything like that about him, and he was to try not to worry about it. Jim also told Joe as they drove out to the house that he and I would do anything we could to be of help to Joe. Jim said we would be happy to go out to his house each morning when Joe left for work, even if it meant getting there at 6 a.m. Between us, he said, we could stay with the children until it was time for them to get up and then get them ready for school and drop them off. We were willing to do whatever we could to help, but sadly for the kids it never came to anything.

Meanwhile, I had travelled out with Paul and Denise in their car, and when we arrived at the house, Jim, Joe and Joe's friend Ciaran Lawlor were already there. I was dreading having to go into the house again. I felt that same terrible coldness as I entered, a feeling I would get every time I went there, right up to the last time I entered the house. Joe had been adamant from the start that he wanted to return to live there with the children. Jim had asked him was he sure that's what he wanted, that he should give it some thought, but Joe said he had thought it through and was set on return- ing. Bearing in mind that this was just two days after the funeral, we were shocked, especially be- cause the house was still in the condition it was in after all the forensic testing. We were informed that there is a service that the police provide to get the scene of a crime cleaned up, but Joe did not want to wait for that, he wanted to move back in as soon as he could, so Jim offered to clean it up with some of our extended family for him.

I decided to first strip off all of the beds and gather up all of the clothes we could find – Rachel's, Joe's, and the children's – as well as all the towels. The majority of the clothes were clean but were scattered about with many other things in the house as part of the 'botched robbery' scene. It was after the murder when the police were finished with the house that I first really saw the condition it had been left in after the forensic testing. I wanted to try to put it back to normal and I felt that, if things were laundered and put away, it would help, as if putting things back in order in the house would have a positive effect. We had lots of black plastic bags, as the bed clothes alone filled a good few. At this time, Joe asked us would we like to hear the phone messages on the answering machine from the day of the murder. No one seemed to answer him and, unprompted, he then started to go through what he thought the murderer would have done at the scene.

Paul, Denise, Jim and I were in their bedroom, and blood still covered the walls, ceiling and surrounding surfaces, although the forensics team had removed the bedroom door frame and taken it away along with some other doors, the trap away from underneath the kitchen sink and the mixer tap, as well as the door to the washing machine. In these surreal surroundings, Joe started to physically re-enact what he claimed the murderer would have done, blow by blow, even going so far as to crouch down as he played it out and make reference to some of the blood splatter on the walls. But it was the look on his face, his manner and the level of detail he produced that shocked us so much. I could no longer take in the words I was hearing. I just wanted him to stop, but he continued his ghastly act over in the bathroom. By this time, I had stopped listening altogether, as his actions and the look on his face were making me feel ill. Paul and Denise were most upset by what Joe was saying in the bathroom, that the killer must have heard Rachel moaning when he got to here and then he went back to finish her off – they only repeated it to us afterwards because they assumed we had heard him, too. We were feeling quite sick at this stage, and I remember thinking to myself, 'This is not happening.'

As we finally made our way back up the hall towards the kitchen, he once again asked did anyone want to hear the answering machine. Again no one answered, and he proceeded to play it. We were still in shock after Joe's re-enactment of the crime when the various messages from the day of the murder started to play. I wondered as they were replayed why Joe so wanted us to hear them. A lot of the messages were from Joe himself, but there was a returned call from Kelsey, a friend of Rachel's in Australia. It seemed that he had phoned her on the day of Rachel's murder to tell her about the murder and to give her his version of what had happened. She hadn't been at home when he called, so he had left a message on her machine, and she had phoned back. Kelsey had been one of Rachel's bridesmaids and was very distressed and upset at her friend's brutal murder. I thought it very odd that Joe had phoned her on the day of the murder – I could never have contacted a casual friend with the news on that very same day, let alone contact someone in a different time zone on the other side of the world, as I was far too upset.

As we stood there listening, Joe was looking intently at each one of us in turn, and, as we waited for the recordings to end, I could hear Rachel's voice quite clearly in my mind. 'Mam, he did it,' she said, as if she was standing right there next to me. I was in shock and, even now, I know I was trying to block it out, but her voice continued: 'I'm telling you, Mam, it was him, he did it.' All my niggling doubts and my sinking feeling about Joe's behaviour since the murder now made sense, and I left Rachel's home that day knowing that Joe had murdered her.

Even though I knew in my bones what had happened, I was trying to see it some other way, and I tried to counter every question in my mind by giving him the benefit of the doubt. We finished cleaning the house as best we could, and Paul and Denise filled their car with the black bags of clothes, even filling the backs of the seats. Jim and I had intended on travelling home in Paul's car with them, but Ciaran Lawlor offered us a lift, and we brought the rest of the black bags with us. Denise took some home with her, and I looked after the rest, and as we laundered the clothes we folded them and gave a few bags back to Joe at a time until they were all finished.

*

I did not say anything to Jim about what I had experienced in Baldarragh until we were back at home. Jim was very disturbed by the re-enactment and was still very upset by it, but I knew I had to tell him. I explained what had happened, that Rachel had spoken to me, and told him that I now felt certain that Joe had murdered our daughter. He was very shocked and implored me not to repeat what I had said to anybody. I remember him telling me that what I had experienced was the result of shock and that Joe's reactions were also as a result of shock. Jim said that nobody can know how he feels, a young man left with two young children in appalling circumstances, and he asked me to try to put these thoughts out of my head. 'There is no way Joe could have done such a thing.' Jim begged me to believe him. Jim said that Joe would have to be the best actor in the world to have done what I was describing – and now we know that indeed he is.

8. Facing the Truth on National Television

Joe rang our house two and a half weeks after Rachel's murder to say that he had been contacted by *The Late Late Show*, enquiring as to whether we would appear on the show the next Friday night. The idea was to keep the story of Rachel's murder in the forefront of people's minds, and to appeal to the public for information. We agreed to do it, and it was arranged that a car would pick up Joe first, then Sarah Harmon, Rachel's neighbour, and then come to our house to collect Jim, Ann and myself. The journey out to Montrose was bizarre, because Joe was acting as if he hadn't a care in the world. When we arrived, the whole party stayed together in the green room, waiting to go on. We were quite comfortable, and there were refreshments provided along with tea, coffee and sandwiches, and a lovely woman called Angela came in periodically to see if we needed anything. Joe was having no problem helping himself to the food they had put out for us that night, and eventually Angela had to bring us more. He had always had a great appetite, but it was an embarrassment to witness his behaviour that night. The circumstances certainly did not affect his appetite in any way, but between the nerves and the upset, the rest of us could barely manage to get anything down.

Just before the show started, Jim, Ann and Sarah Harmon had to go down and join the audience. Joe and I were left alone together with only Angela, the hostess, coming in from time to time to provide us with yet more sandwiches and hot drinks. The whole time we were there, Joe was texting non-stop and once or twice he made reference to a friend. Whoever the friend was, they had him chuckling a lot, but in between texts, he was watching Tommy Tiernan on the monitor, as the comedian was also appearing on the show that night. Compared to Joe, I must have appeared too sombre, because eventually he looked over at me and said, 'He is an acquired taste, Rose.' Eventually we were brought down to appear on the show, and I was grateful to get out of that room and do what we had come to do.

It was 22 October, less than three weeks since Rachel had been murdered. I sat to Pat Kenny's left, and Joe sat on my left. Pat Kenny was on the edge of his seat. I noticed that Joe wasn't wearing his wedding ring – it had not taken him long to discard it, which we had first realized when we were making the funeral arrangements. It was very hard to keep my composure as the cameras rolled, as it had only been nine days since I had left Rachel's house knowing in my very bones that Joe was the murderer – and there he was on national television, sitting right beside me. I just about got through the interview that the whole of Ireland is familiar with by now. In addition to that, I was still trying to come to terms with how I felt – both being convinced that I had to trust my instincts and, on the other hand, hating myself for having such awful thoughts and trying to justify the very strange behaviour that Joe continued to display. The Gardaí had been keeping us informed about significant developments in their investigation and by now they had told us that Joe O'Reilly had been having an affair. Even though he had said we would hear stories about him having an affair, when the Gardaí told us that it was a fact, it was a huge shock. I just could not believe it. Around the same time, someone who had a connection to him through work told us that we should be aware that there was talk about him having an affair with a colleague called Nikki Pelley. Even knowing all this, on that night out at *The Late Late Show*, I was still wrestling with the truth, willing things to be different. It was as if every thought in my mind was up for interrogation, and I kept being pulled this way and that. I just could not bear to face the truth.

As I sat there, I remember being very angry at him for putting on such an act, but I tried to remain calm, and so the nightmare went on. Pat asked Joe what kind of a woman Rachel had been, and Joe's answer in that now-familiar, flat tone of his caused me physical pain: 'Just a normal woman,' he said, blandly. He went on to describe some of the things she had done, describing Rachel as a 'mother of two small children, nothing out of the ordinary, no lifestyle of the rich and famous', he quipped glibly. 'Just an ordinary person,' he said of his beautiful young wife. I was furious to hear him call Rachel 'just an ordinary person'. In the glare of the lights, things were beginning to appear clearer to me. I remember not wanting to touch him and feeling bad about it, but Joe's words were helping to chip away at my doubts, and I was angry and heart-broken all at once. The monster was beginning to emerge, and his arrogance led him to believe that he had gotten away with it. Even as Pat asked how they met, and how he proposed, Joe never spoke one word of love for Rachel – as ever, I was waiting for words that never came. As the interview went on, some of what Joe said wasn't true. He did not meet Rachel at softball, as he claimed, but at Arnott's. Some of the lies weren't known to us then, like when Pat asked about plans for Rachel's birthday, we didn't know that Joe never had any intention of going out for a meal with his wife as he said he did, but we would learn more about it as time went on. I thought back to her last birthday with sadness, knowing that he had ruined it for her by being away in Florida, failing even to ring her and coming home with the witch's outfit. It just put it all in a much bigger context.

By the time he started to describe his out-of-body experience on seeing her body and his instinct 'just kicking in', I felt sick. I knew he was lying as he spoke, and it took all of my strength not to react as he continued, devoid of emotion, to tell the nation about the paramedics with their 'box of tricks' and 'electric shock things'. He was performing and he was enjoying it. He switched tactics and began

to plant his poisonous suspicion when Pat asked
him, 'Was the murderer perhaps someone Rachel
trusted?' 'Yes, I think so,' he replied confidently.
'Where the murder happened was in the bedroom,
which is the very last room of the house,' he said. 'It
would be the last place she would bring someone
she did not know because she would be cornered.'
Joe kept underlining the idea that she knew the
person. My own personal view is that she certainly
did know this person. My view is, he lured her
down to the bedroom somehow – it would not have
been hard to do, as Rachel trusted him. I think he
was most probably hiding behind the door and
he took her by surprise. Her body showed marks on
her neck that could have come from being caught
in an arm lock and marks on her wrists consistent
with being held by the wrist so as she could not
move her arm. Coward that he is, he used the
element of surprise, and had it well thought out
and researched before he committed the murder.
He even explained how hard it would have been to
get someone of Rachel's size and fitness down
on the ground. Despite his cowardice, he seemed
to have no fear of getting caught as he described
exactly what he had done to her. As he described
what 'they must have done' to her, I could visualize
him actually doing it as I sat there beside him. His

telling of what he did after overcoming Rachel will haunt me for ever.

What was going on in my head at that point in time is very hard to convey properly. On one level, I really was trying not to think of Joe as the murderer, as it was so horrific to come to terms with, so my thoughts were constantly conflicted. At times it just seemed that I was having a terrible nightmare from which I couldn't wake up. Try as I might, I could not deny what was becoming increasingly clear. I knew that the details he was revealing live on national television just weren't true, and the more Joe spoke, the more questions were raised in my mind. As the interview continued, it was impossible for me not to notice the offhand references he made to Rachel, as if he was speaking about someone for whom he had no feelings whatsoever. I have watched that interview again since, and I can see the cloud of doubt growing over me during the course of the show.

When it was over, we were brought back up to the green room. Joe's family phoned to congratulate him on the interview, and our family stayed on and had a chat with various people until Pat came up and spent some time with us. Joe did not wait around for long, saying that he had to go to meet some American friends. It was a business arrangement, and, he explained, it had been pre-arranged. It was almost midnight at this point, and it sounded a bit strange to have a business arrangement so late. I had my own ideas about that, and I turned out to be right. I knew straight away that there was no business meeting – common sense told me that American businessmen who had been travelling would not be holding meetings after midnight, and common sense told me what it might have been. I wasn't quite sure what he was up to, but I was certain that what he wanted us to believe was a lie. Jim asked him where the meeting was to be, and Joe said it was in Rathfarnham. The same driver was leaving him out as was taking us back home again, so I guess that Joe knew if he lied about the destination, we would find out. As it is well known now, his meeting was indeed in Rathfarnham, but at the home of his mistress, Nikki Pelley, where he was to spend the night.

Four weeks after Rachel died, we held a month's mind Mass in Whitehall Church which was attended by family and friends. We were left bewildered as we sat at the front of the church, and the Mass proceeded with no sign of Joe or any members of his family. After the Mass, the priest said, 'Where's

Joe?', but we didn't know. We were later met by Joe and some of his family at the back of the church, who said that they had been delayed by bad traffic. Afterwards, everyone was invited back to our house for refreshments, but Joe and his family declined. This did not go unnoticed by anyone in our family or among our friends.

9. The Chameleon Among Us

From the start of the investigation, Joe told the Gardaí that there were two brown towels and parts from a set of weights missing from his house. The police were working very hard behind the scenes and were following up on every possible lead, so they continued a thorough search for the missing items in the surrounding area. They even had several Gardaí divers spend two days searching a disused quarry near by. They recovered many things from the bottom of the quarry, but there was still no sign of the murder weapon.

Shortly after the investigation started, the contrived burglar theory was now being discounted. The police had found €860 in a plastic box in the utility room, money that Rachel had been collecting for new jerseys for the softball team. In addition to that, there was about €400 in a purse in her bag. Even if the alleged intruder had missed the money in the utility room, it would seem very odd for an actual burglar to overlook that amount of cash in such an obvious place, and instead run off with personal items of Rachel's with virtually no monetary value. The Gardaí had found a video camera, a camera bag, an old handbag and items of jewellery, which they felt fed into the staged robbery theory. They were of the opinion that the items had been placed in such a way as to be seen rather than hidden. Furthermore, there was so much blood involved in the attack that, if thieves had left the house in a hurry that day, they would have left a trail of blood behind them. As the evidence began to unfold, and once every possible suspect had been thoroughly investigated and discounted, it emerged that, far from being a random killing, this murder was beginning to look like a very careful and planned act.

In the middle of all this, I was finding it very difficult to act as if everything was normal when I was around Joe. One part of me knew without a shadow of a doubt that Joe was the murderer, but there was always a part of me that didn't want to accept the truth, as it was just too awful to contemplate. I kept trying to see it some other way, to come up with any reason that he could not possibly have done it, but the more I saw and the more I heard over those days only compounded the truth.

During the weeks that followed Rachel's death there was a media frenzy, and it surrounded more than just Joe being a suspect, and many other details had started to emerge. As hard as it was to handle reporters interviewing us, coming to the house and the phone ringing off the hook, I understood from the very beginning it was a necessary part of the whole nightmare – but it didn't make it any easier. For the most part, the media were as respectful as possible under the circumstances. They had a job to do, but I for my part was very aware that we could not talk to them at all. It was very difficult to refuse continuously to make any comment, and I hoped that they understood that we couldn't risk giving away potential evidence. It was almost impossible to stay focused on doing the right thing by the Gardaí, the solicitors and all of the people who were working so hard to help, because Rachel's name and face were everywhere, which, though it was important to keep the story alive in the minds of the public while the Gardaí gathered evidence, was very hard for us.

There were times when I was out driving and would pass the paper boy at the traffic lights as he held up the front page for all the drivers to see, and Rachel's face would be staring back at me again. Soon, Joe's photograph was being printed as much as Rachel's, and it began to take on a surreal feeling. Their faces had become symbols of the case. Those days, I felt as if I was just sitting in the eye of the storm, with all of this mayhem going on in circles around me. I kept thinking that this was not happening to me, praying to God to help me wake from the nightmare of seeing Rachel's name plastered across the headlines. I remember the time we chose that name for her – a beautiful name for a beautiful little girl. I never knew how well known that name would become, but I take strength from the fact that it will certainly never be forgotten.

From the very start it seemed to us that Joe was too much involved with the press. The Gardaí had advised both Joe and ourselves against talking to the press, for the simple reason that, at a time like that, it was very easy to say the wrong thing, and they told us to be very careful. I remember Joe saying to one of our lads that, whoever the main suspect was, they were going to be able to use all the publicity in their defence. The main suspect had not yet been named then, but Joe had so much to say to the media and had his photograph in the papers so much from talking to reporters, it seemed inevitable that things would soon emerge that did not add up. It was unbelievable to us that he couldn't help himself, that he wanted to remain in the limelight as the husband seeking justice, even though he would later claim that the press attention was part of a set-up.

Looking back, I see that Joe was like a chameleon. He could fit perfectly into the exact role he wished to play and that had many different faces – for us, the press, the public, the court – but the most chilling thing about him was his ability to play all of his roles so well. As Jim often points out to me, we were taken in by him more than anyone. Joe's ability to manipulate situations to his benefit cropped up in many different instances after Rachel's murder. One of my close friends remembers one such time during the wake, when the house was packed with people and Rachel's friends were in and out. Most of the members of the softball team were in the lounge, and others were at the end of the hall that particular day. Joe was on his own with his back to the stairs, facing directly into the lounge, where Rachel's body lay. He stood staring at the large photograph of Rachel as a beautiful bride that we had placed on top of the coffin and said aloud to himself, 'Imagine such a beautiful girl and she can't even have an open coffin.' She said that she felt so sorry for him and was very upset.

But his performance as the grieving widower slipped occasionally, even before Rachel was buried. One of the days of the wake, a friend of the family who had never met Joe came to visit. She saw a very tall man who was standing around chatting with the friends and family, watching everyone come and go. He seemed to be studying the mourners' faces, and so our friend reasonably assumed that the man was a detective on the case – and not the bereaved husband of a woman who had just met a brutal end. She was very shocked when someone pointed Joe out to her and she told us the story afterwards.

Another of those days, I was trying to console him, and he began telling me that there were going to be rumours that he had been having an affair. In fact, he said, they had started already. He turned and looked me in the eye and he said that there would also be rumours about us having abused Rachel. I'd never heard anything so absurd – but now I see that he was only trying to rattle me as he had done Rachel.

He talked a lot about the rumours that were

supposedly flying around about him, particularly about him having an affair. I had heard him say it many times, right from the start, as if he were laying the foundations of a denial. He also told us one day that a friend had phoned him to tell him that he had heard a rumour that Rachel was having an affair. Joe had told him that he didn't think she had been, but even if it was true, there wasn't anything he could do about it now. I was truly shocked by that, as it was the first time since she died that he had cast aspersions on Rachel's character – but it wouldn't be the last. The supposed abuse claims against us were more of the same, further examples of Joe's true nature and how he went about sowing seeds of doubt, as he made out that he wasn't the only one to be wrongly accused by rumours.

Soon before he was arrested, Joe was in our home to pick up our son Anthony to see a film, and he was discussing the recent media reports. At this stage, he was clearly feeling the heat from the press and said from the start to Anthony and anyone else who would listen that he was the chief suspect in Rachel's murder. After all, he would say, nine times out of ten, it's the husband, partner or someone very close to the victim who is responsible. He would usually attribute that quote to someone else, while trying to make the point that it was perfectly normal for him to be a suspect until they found the murderer, or more importantly, until the Gardaí could rule him out completely. He made it out to be standard procedure, as if the media were excited over nothing. He also remarked to Jim, Ann and me that some people just do not seem to value human life. I didn't know what to make of that, whether he was talking about Rachel's murderer or about the media throwing accusations at him, but I could not even look at him let alone ask him questions. I just wanted him to go. He was never to visit us after that evening.

10. The Biggest Murder Investigation in the History of the State

As the investigation continued, so did Joe O'Reilly's strange behaviour. It is well documented that Joe invited the media to the house to give interviews, and to take reporters on 'The Tour', as he called it so insensitively. It would seem that he had no idea how to behave normally, even when the stakes were so high, but clearly he didn't think that he was in any danger. His behaviour might even have gone unnoticed had he not spoken to so many journalists and given so many interviews. As they went along, the press would take photographs and listen to Joe's version of events. After one such tour, he told one journalist that he was tired of crying, but seeing as they were about to take pictures, he asked, 'Would you like me to cry now?' He seemed to think he was untouchable as he continued to revel in the attention he was attracting. He proclaimed openly that he was a suspect, but repeated by way of explanation that eight or nine out of ten murdered women are killed by their partners. He point blank denied having an affair – not once but on several occasions – and when he finally realized the truth was out, he insisted it was over. But later through evidence in court we learned that there had been at least eighteen communications by mobile phone between Joe and his mistress on the day of the murder. The first call from his lover, Nikki Pelley, was at 05.45 a.m. that morning and lasted for 27 minutes and 43 seconds, and the last communication between them was also from Nikki Pelley, at 18.56 that evening. It was quite clear that Joe was lying when he said it was over.

The Gardaí were working around the clock every day, gathering as much evidence as they could, and collected hundreds of witness statements. Superintendent Tom Gallagher led over sixty officers in the biggest murder investigation in the history of the Irish state. They set about making inquiries at every house in a ten-mile radius of Lambay View and checking every home and business on the journey between Rachel's house and the bus depot where Joe said he had been at the time of the murder. The police checked every rubbish skip from the house all along that road, thinking that the murder weapon could have been dumped on the way, but without success. That key piece of evidence has never been found. They left nothing to chance, and the two detectives we got to know through the whole ordeal, Detectives Pat Marry and Peter McCoy, were representative of the way all the men worked on Rachel's case. We discovered first-hand how very dedicated and selfless the Gardaí really are, as we saw that at no point were they prepared to give up.

Their hard work and compassion is something for which we will always be grateful. I was so low and helpless sometimes, wondering if justice would ever be done, but when Detectives Pat Marry and Peter McCoy would call into our house to give us an update or check in, by the time they would leave, our spirits would have lifted and we'd be hopeful once more. Those two men, and so many like them, work far beyond the call of duty, and we, the public at large, are totally oblivious to it. I was only sorry that we had to learn this under such dreadful conditions, but I will never forget all of those men and women who worked on Rachel's case.

*

At first, Joe O'Reilly's cunning plan seemed to be working. Joe was now trying to be very convincing in his role of the bereaved husband, but thank God it was not long before his lies began to trip him up. He is so callous that it is clearly hard for him to show feelings that he is incapable of having, so his carefully prepared plan began to unravel. A few things had been glaringly obvious from the beginning, first and foremost being the lack of any unknown DNA at the scene despite the sickening amount of blood. Every person who had been in Rachel's house that day had given a DNA sample and yet no one else's DNA was found – not in blood, hair or foreign fibres. Straight away, the evidence suggested that either no one else was in the house that day, or that whoever did commit the horrific murder planned it meticulously – or both.

It became apparent that Joe could well have had the opportunity to commit the murder. He would have known how unlikely it was that he would be disturbed, and of course Rachel would have trusted him and would have been lured into the trap he had created in the bedroom. If he had timed it all with calm precision, he could have showered off any evidence before driving away. What also attracted attention was that the items that the alleged burglar had left in the ditch beside the house had no blood on them, as it would have been impossible for the killer to have handled them without leaving blood or fingerprints behind, and there was not a trace of either to be found on any of the items. (Our Ann was so upset when these were produced as evidence during the trial. The sum total of her treasures was not worth very much, and it summed up how little she really did have – yet Rachel had been worth so much more. She never asked for much for herself, and it was clear that she had not been given much, when she gave so much to her husband and family.)

On top of the lack of evidence to support the intruder theory, Joe had been seen behaving strangely the day of the murder. Joe claimed that he had returned to his office in Bluebell after inspecting buses at the Broadstone depot all morning. Joe also claimed that he and his colleague Derek Quearney had finished up their work at about 11.30 a.m. and headed back to work in separate cars, arriving in Bluebell at about midday, before Rachel's body was found. The receptionist from Joe's place of work told the detectives that, when Joe returned to the office, he looked like he had been crying and was looking flustered. She remembered saying to him, 'You look like shit.' To which he muttered, 'Ah Jaysus . . .' He went into his office with a cup of coffee, probably under the impression that, so far, he had gotten away with it.

As part of his elaborate plan for the murder, he had made a lunch date with a friend of his to give the appearance of it being a normal day. During the trial, we learned that he had arranged to meet Kieran Gallagher for lunch, and to make sure that his friend would not try to contact him while he was in the middle of murdering his wife, Joe sent him an email early that morning confirming the lunch date. He told Kieran not to bother trying to contact him as he would be out and about during the morning and would not have good mobile coverage, and that he would meet him for lunch as arranged. What Joe did not realize was that his friend's young daughter was ill that morning, and Kieran did not go to work but stayed at home with his sick child. As a result, he never got Joe's email and texted Joe to cancel the lunch date. The irony of it was that Kieran's text was one of the communications that registered on Joe's phone at the time of the murder via the mast at Murphy's Quarry, just up the road from the house where he battered his wife to death. This was just one of many mobile phone communications that were to expose this arrogant murderer, and with the help of CCTV evidence his whereabouts could be completely verified.

Six weeks after the murder, on 16 November, Derek Quearney, who was a friend of Joe's as well as being his colleague, and Joe's mistress, Nikki Pelley, were arrested on suspicion of withholding information in previous statements. Quearney was arrested in Ballyfermot at 10 a.m. and taken to Drogheda Garda Station for questioning, and Pelley was arrested about an hour later in Dundrum, and later taken to Balbriggan Garda Station for questioning. Pelley and Quearney were held under Section 30 of the Offences Against the State Act, which meant that they could be held without charge for up to seventy-two hours, and both were still in custody when Joe was arrested in Baldarragh at approximately ten the following morning.

To me, it was what he did not say when he was questioned that revealed the most. When I heard of his arrest I requested a visit with him in Drogheda Garda Station. I wanted to see him face to face, as I wanted to somehow represent Rachel now that she was gone. The visit was sanctioned, and Jim drove me up to Drogheda. Joe had agreed to see me, and I was shown into a small room with Joe, and a police officer was present. I do not know what Joe was expecting, but when I sat down opposite to him, I told him that, as Rachel had never been allowed a voice in all of this, I was here now as her voice. He didn't seem to react much at all, so I continued. I asked him if he realized what he had done, and he sat looking at me blankly. I reminded him that he had denied that he had a mistress and he had denied murdering Rachel, and I did not believe him. I spoke to him for some time, but it was plain that I was getting nowhere. I suppose I thought that I would get him to admit what he had done, or at least say something. I told him that there is a price to pay for our actions, and I hoped that his had been worth it. His last words to me as I got up to go were 'I am sorry.' Things changed drastically between us after that visit, as all pretence of his innocence was put aside. He knew that I knew he did it. When he realized the game was up in relation to us, that he could no longer hoodwink us, he gave up even trying. It was then that we began to experience the real Joe O'Reilly.

Joe was released, having been held for questioning under Section 4 of the Criminal Justice Act for almost twelve hours. Joe had refused to answer questions or to speak of Rachel's murder to the press in any way after it became apparent he was being treated as a suspect, and when he left

Drogheda with his brother Derek in a blaze of publicity, he still had no comment to make. Nikki Pelley and Derek Quearney were also released without charge that evening. Joe would later claim that he was thrown to the wolves and had been encouraged to give interviews by the Gardaí, when we all knew that the opposite was the case.

11. Joe O'Reilly's Double Life

In the weeks before and after Rachel's murder, Joe was lying to everyone about Rachel and about every aspect of their life. I know now that lying for him was just a way of life, and he accepted as normal things that most of us would never consider. Rachel would never have been suspicious or distrustful of anything he did or told her, so he thought that he had got away with it all. If he could have sustained his double life, who knows how long it would have gone on for? Alternatively, if Rachel had discovered his double life, how would things have been different? It's hard to know how anything could have changed the terrible outcome, because Joe felt entitled to live the way he did, and he thought he deserved more – it was a kind of fantasy that he had created. He never gave a thought to his loyal and loving wife, but, rather, seemed to feel that his need for an adulterous relationship and all the deceit that went with it was actually Rachel's fault.

During the trial it was revealed that, before Rachel died, Joe's mistress was getting impatient and let him know quite clearly that she was not prepared to go along with things as they were for much longer. We learned through court testimony that Nikki Pelley had given Joe an ultimatum that he had to leave Rachel by November 2004 in order to continue a relationship with her. I think that it was then that he became very hostile towards Rachel.

I cannot be sure if or when Rachel became aware of all this, or how much she suspected, but now I know that she was not happy towards the end of her life. I have often heard the term 'domestic abuse', but it usually refers to physical violence in the home. I do not know if Joe O'Reilly was physically abusive to Rachel – he may have tried, but she would have defended herself. But there are other kinds of abuse that occur between partners, and there is nothing more sinister than the kind of psychological abuse which causes a person's perception of their entire life to change. As we learned during the trial, Rachel was being psychologically abused by her husband. She would have been aware of the very negative undercurrents in her relationship with Joe, but it would have been hard for her to understand what was happening, as Joe was still playing the role of the family man. Outwardly, his life with Rachel looked normal, as they attended a family fair with the children a matter of weeks before she was murdered, and she was looking forward to the promised holiday to Canada in the New Year.

While playing the part of the good husband to Rachel, in March of 2004, Joe had organized a family holiday to Canada to see a relative of his. The holiday was to start on New Year's Eve 2004. Rachel was so looking forward to that family holiday and had already shown me some clothes she had bought for the children, beautiful little outfits she was never to see them wear. She had also been collecting things for herself and Joe. She was so excited when she talked about it and was looking forward to her kids seeing so much snow for the first time in their young lives. She anticipated how much fun they would have sitting in sleighs and building snowmen with them. Sadly, by New Year's Eve, Rachel was lying in a cold grave.

I wonder about that holiday, and it still doesn't

make sense to me. Why would he have booked it in the first place? Why bother playing happy families to that extent? Thinking back, I remember one day during the summer of 2004, when Rachel was in our kitchen with myself and the children. I was passing some remark to them about their upcoming holiday in the snow and how great it was going to be, when Rachel jumped behind them and indicated by waving her hands I was not to tell them about the holiday. At the time they were too young to pay much attention, so it just passed over their heads. Rachel was very relieved they had not found out and explained to me that Joe did not want them to know about the holiday until the time came. I didn't know why he wouldn't have wanted to tell them, as children always get as big a kick out of the anticipation as they do out of the event itself when it comes to something fun like a holiday. Something about that trip has always felt odd to me, just another indication of things not being right. I do not think Joe ever intended to take Rachel to Canada, but we will never know.

The holiday was only part of the picture of happy family life that Joe was trying to maintain. Around the same time as I learned that the children weren't to know about the trip to Canada, there was a christening in our family for Declan and Denise's son, Sam, which was attended by Joe, Rachel and the two children. It was not until after Rachel's death that we learned of the false allegations that were made against Rachel to the Child Protection Services in June 2004, meaning that she knew that her parenting was in doubt throughout all of these family occasions. We were further horrified to discover during the trial that it was Joe's mother, Anne O'Reilly, who had contacted Child Services about Rachel when emails dated June 2004 were read to the court.

Joe's double life continued to have many facets. In addition to playing the family man while supporting false abuse allegations against his wife, he was also balancing celebrations with our family of his children's milestones with his plan to raise their children alone with his mistress. On their eldest's first day of school in late August 2004, Rachel, Joe and the children arrived unexpectedly at our house to show us the new school uniform. Ann and I were having lunch in Drumcondra and we asked them to join us, but they declined, as Joe was in a hurry. It emerged in court that Joe had sent Nikki Pelley a text that night: 'Just to text you. Our child's first school day. Had fun but will have lots of homework tomorrow. Love you.' It was deeply upsetting for us to hear him describe

Rachel's child to his mistress as 'our child'. It was yet another moment in the trial when we thought it couldn't get any worse, but it did. The revelation that Joe O'Reilly had begun to describe Rachel's child as belonging to him and his mistress was so painful, so shocking, that we could barely take it in. The most cruel part was that Rachel had been so looking forward to this day, which had been so important to her as one of her eldest child's first big milestones.

Our Ann spoke to Rachel on the Friday night before her murder, to see what her plans were for the weekend. Rachel was excited, telling Ann that Joe was taking her to Liffey Valley on the Sunday afternoon – 3 October, a full week before her actual birthday on 10 October – to buy her her birthday present. Joe had made a string of plans in advance, which included the trip to Liffey Valley, and, later, to contact Rachel's half-brother Thomas. It was not until after Rachel's death that we discovered that she had looked up her birth mother when she was eighteen, and that she had recently begun to have contact with the Lowes again, but paying Thomas a visit that Sunday evening was again part of Joe's plan to appear as a normal, functioning family. As time passed and the trial unfolded, we learned that this kind of manipulation was typical of the lengths Joe would go to in order to cover his tracks.

Joe's carefully thought-out plan to prepare people for the revelations about his affair had also failed. Even though I was quite sure that Joe was a murderer, it was still shocking to find out for certain that he had a mistress – it was the last thing I would have expected, and I just could not take it in. Finally, I could understand his coldness and the way he avoided our family in the months before he carried out his brutal act, why Rachel was alone in the house so much, and even why Joe had been trying so hard to play at happy families.

Barely three weeks after Rachel's murder was her youngest child's third birthday. Rachel had made plans to do something special, as birthdays were always very important to her. The morning of the birthday, Joe's brother Derek was in our house with his son, along with Joe and the kids. Jim, Ann, my sons and their children, and myself were all there. We had a cake with candles on it and we tried as best we could to make a small party. The little one opened the presents, with eyes lighting up as everyone clapped and sang along, but my heart broke for what that child had lost. I was pleased that Joe had organized a group of friends to go to the

Leisureplex that afternoon – I knew the children would love that. He had invited some of the children's mums to accompany their kids as well. A few weeks later, one of Rachel's friends who had attended showed us the photos that she had taken. We knew most of the people there, but she pointed out a friend of Joe's, Nikki Pelley. I had heard that name by now and was sickened at the thought that, on *this*, one of Rachel's special days, Joe could bring his mistress along to celebrate the day his wife had given birth to his baby.

This was the same birthday that Joe described to the journalist Jenny Friel as being so upsetting because Rachel wasn't there, making him feel like a basket case. But Joe had planned who he wanted to be there for the child's birthday, and it was not his wife.

I do not know towards the end how much Rachel did know or how much she suspected about Joe's affair, but I can only imagine that it must have been a painful time for her, and that the pressure she was experiencing must have been unbearable. During the trial, we got just a glimpse of the feelings displayed towards her by Joe, and after the email evidence between Joe and his sister Anne O'Reilly Jnr was read aloud it still makes feel sick at the thought of them coming into our home. I am now aware of the awful names that he called his wife, so God only knows what he was saying about Rachel to his family and friends. Did people who had never met or spoken to Rachel form their opinion on his word alone? It seems unbelievable that they would, for any man who would describe the mother of his children as he did can't have been considered to be a very good father or husband. Yet the circumstances have to be right for Joe's mask to slip, so perhaps people who didn't know him well were none the wiser. After all, Jim and I had known him for thirteen years, and we really knew nothing about him except what he wanted us to believe. He was chillingly good at doing that.

12. The Torturous Road to Justice

On many different occasions over the next few months, we heard rumours of supposed break-throughs, only to find that it was not so. Everyone we met during this time tried to help by asking if we had seen the latest headline, or heard the news that day; whenever there was anything about Rachel's murder in the paper it was generally either old news, or unconfirmed reports. It was terrible when we got our hopes up at first, but we came to realize that it was nothing more than the media wanting a story to report. These misunderstandings were part and parcel of the nightmare that nobody could control. Sometimes, though, the reports flagged up new developments that were interesting to us. Not long after Joe's arrest, we heard about a new kind of technology that could locate a mobile phone and that the proof it provided was indisputable. We knew that it put Joe's phone in the vicinity of the house in Baldarragh at the time of his wife's death, as Joe had already admitted that his phone was with him at all times that day. I thought back to Joe's own message to Rachel's murderer on one of the television interviews: 'It is only a matter of time until you are caught.' He was right – time and technology were catching up on him.

The media speculation continued as the Gardaí worked diligently on the case, and we continued to place our absolute trust in them. When the detectives called in to our house during that time, I would question them on everything, although they could only let us know so much. It must have been hard on them as well, as I'm sure they could see that we were living for a breakthrough, but they were doing all that was humanly possible to bring the culprit to justice.

The first inquest was held on 8 March 2005, the same day that Rachel's body was being exhumed. The police had been given information about the letters and cards that were put into Rachel's coffin, and they needed to see if they contained any relevant evidence towards the case, so we gave them permission to exhume her body. Jim and I had decided to attend the inquest, rather than the exhumation, which had been arranged just a few days before. We were in the car just before we reached the courthouse in Tallaght when we heard on the radio that the Gardaí had recovered evidence from Rachel's coffin. We learned later that a letter had been retrieved, but was in very bad condition and had to be taken to experts at Garda Headquarters in the Phoenix Park, where it could be restored well enough to be read.

At the inquest, Jim and I found Dr Marie Cassidy's evidence of Rachel's injuries very hard to take. Although I had seen myself what had been done to her, it was another thing altogether to hear it described out loud – it made the horror of Rachel's final moments all too real to us. Even the less disturbing evidence was upsetting, as it was revealed in her autopsy report that Rachel had nothing in her stomach – that was typical of Rachel, as it meant that she had fed the children their breakfast and not eaten herself. She always thought of herself last and her children first, down to the day she was killed. We hoped now more than ever that her killer would be caught. Joe was not there at the inquest that morning, but a friend of his, Ciaran Lawlor, was there, and towards the end of the hearing Joe's brother Derek arrived. The inquest was then postponed for a further six months.

It was the beginning of a torturous journey for us of waiting and hoping. Headlines would appear from time to time that would get our hopes up, only for them to be dashed again. Rachel's murder had aroused so much public interest that the scope of the information was hard to take in, but following the legalities of the case was even harder. We were very disturbed to discover that Rachel's death certificate had been issued shortly after that first inquest – it is most unusual to issue a death certificate when the deceased is a murder victim whose spouse is the chief suspect. The reason for this is that no insurance monies can be paid out or mortgage protection policies collected until a death certificate is produced. Legally, no one is permitted to make any financial gain in the event of such a death until a verdict is found and the guilty parties identified. We were shocked to learn that Joe had obtained one, and still to this day we have not been given an explanation as to how that did happen.

In October 2005, for the first anniversary of her death, we decided to have a vigil outside Rachel's house. A vigil served one very personal important purpose for us: to show her that she was loved.

I am very aware of how she met a horrific death, and I could feel the hatred shown to her in her dying moments the first time I saw her battered body – a cold chill that reached my very bones. Rachel needed to know that she was not alone, and we would never forget her. I am plagued by constant visions of that morning Joe had planned so meticulously. I see Rachel so young, vibrant and beautiful, having just left her two babies for the last time.

I can imagine Rachel's happy smile as she realized Joe was in the house, wondering why he was home. I wonder how he got her to come down to the bedroom, and I try desperately to let go at that point – but I picture Rachel smiling up at him, looking into his evil eyes. The terror she must have felt at what she saw in those eyes. Did she realize she was in the presence of such evil? Did she plead with him for her life? Did she beg him to spare her for the sake of their children? Did she know right away what was to come? The very idea of the terror she must have felt when she realized that her husband had come home to murder her will always have the power to tear at my heart, which is torturous. On *The Late Late Show*, Joe had said how hard it would have been to get her down. He made reference to how fit and strong she was, and the job that 'they' would have had. It was revealed during the trial that Joe was of course right – Rachel had tried to defend herself. Had she looked into the eyes of the one she had trusted with her life and happiness, only to see the pure and utter hatred he felt for her? I am quite sure the thoughts of leaving her babies in the hands of this monster were uppermost in her mind as she tried to fight for her life.

All of this compelled me to prepare for the vigil for her first anniversary in 2005, but Jim wasn't up to it, and I understood. A year later, at the time of her second anniversary in 2006, we were all ready to mark the day. It was a Wednesday afternoon and, we hoped, a quiet enough time in the week to hold the vigil outside Rachel's home on the road-way. Very early on the morning of the vigil, Jim and Paul went down to The Naul to erect signs that they had made directing people to the house, putting them up all the way from off the slip road to where the vigil was to be held. We were very moved at the number of friends, family and total strangers that attended that day – the news reported that there were several hundred people there – and yet there was not a sign of any of the O'Reilly family. It was a lovely service, and we were so grateful to Father Tom, Joe McNally and his singing group and all of the people that came to show their support. Rachel was there among us that day and would have been very touched by it all.

Between the vigil and Rachel's birthday less than a week later, many flowers arrived at our home. On the day of her birthday, we brought all the flowers out to her grave, and I tied some helium Disney balloons to her cross, as Rachel was a great Disney fan. By the time we had finished, her grave was covered in colourful flowers, and the balloons were waving and glistening in the sun. It was a beautiful, dry but cold day, and we could not help but feel sad to think that she was already in her grave on her thirty-third birthday. Ann even took some photographs of the grave before we left as it looked so lovely.

Two days later, I got a call from my friend, Val, who asked if we had been out to Rachel's grave. Val's daughter, Anita, was one of Rachel's best childhood friends, and she and her mother had gone to the cemetery to bring Rachel flowers for her birthday. They remarked to each other on the number of flowers and how beautiful Rachel's grave looked but now, little more than a day later, Val had gone back after a neighbour's funeral to find the grave stripped and bare. We were appalled to hear this and went out ourselves. Sure enough, everything had been removed and thrown in the rubbish skip near by – we even have photographs of the beautiful fresh flowers dumped. Families would often dispose of dead flowers, but our photographs show perfectly good fresh ones thrown in among the rubbish. All that remained of her birthday balloons was a piece of severed coloured ribbon blowing in the breeze around the cross. I just feel so desolate at times when I picture Rachel lying in her grave with her young life cruelly cut short. I know she could have achieved so much. I picture our beautiful girl who could have picked a dream, any dream, and made it come true. The utter waste of such a valuable and loving spirit is hard to come to terms with, and this further act of destruction was one of the most upsetting things we have had to endure, as, even in her grave, Rachel was being violated.

Just over one week after the vigil, on 19 October 2006, Joe O'Reilly was arrested again and charged with the murder of his wife but was released on bail pending the trial. Shortly afterwards, the date for the trial was set for June 2007. We were just so relieved that it was actually going to happen, that we were making progress, that maybe we would get some closure and be able to move on with our lives. The ordinary people of Ireland came out in support of justice in great numbers, which was extremely moving, particularly as it was two years since Rachel had died. We had beautiful letters and cards with messages of support and Mass cards from complete strangers who will never know how much they have helped us. It made us realize that when two and two does not make seventeen, the ordinary decent public out there can see it for themselves, and no amount of conniving is going to convince them otherwise.

13. The Trial Gets Off to a Nerve-racking Start

The few months leading up to the trial were very stressful, and time seemed to slow to a standstill, but eventually the time was upon us. Just a few days before the trial was due to begin, the Gardaí arrived at the house to tell us that it had been postponed – it would now be a week later, as the judge had other commitments. We were devastated by even a small setback like this, but decided to use the time to prepare for what was to come. We had previously made contact with Victim Support, and the two ladies we had spoken to, Pat Hannah and Phyl Costello, came out to visit us on a few occasions in the weeks prior to the trial. They suggested that we all meet at the courts on the day the trial was due to begin so that they could show us around and we could familiarize ourselves with the surroundings. It was very helpful to know a little bit of what to expect in terms of practicalities, particularly because I was very nervous every day for the next week, for fear that the trial would be put back again for some reason. We had been told that, although another delay did not seem likely, it was entirely possible. Thank God there were no more hitches, and the trial began. Pat Hannah and Phyl Costello never left our sides, staying with us every day and giving us their unwavering support for the next four weeks. We are so grateful to them for everything.

We will never forget the night before the trial was to begin. It was a long, restless night for all of us, and we got up early the next morning. We had ordered a taxi for the first day of the trial, as my brother Charlie's taxi was being serviced, so it was a stressful start to a very difficult day. We had all steeled ourselves for what lay before us on that first morning, but nothing could prepare you for the experience of walking through a battery of cameras to get inside the gates of the court.

The Round Hall of the Four Courts was packed that morning, but we could not help but notice Joe O'Reilly sitting on one of the benches along the hall, casually reading a newspaper. His application for bail had been successful at the time he was charged, so he had been walking around as a free man ever since. We tried to sit as far from him as possible as we waited for the door of Court Number 2 to open. He looked so disconnected from the whole scene that one could have been for-given for mistaking him for a casual onlooker. His demeanour changed when he made his way into the courtroom, and he looked quite businesslike. You had to wonder what part he thought he was playing as he carried his folder stuffed with papers under his arm and took his place immediately facing where the jury would sit. He did his best to avoid looking anybody in the eye and kept himself busy going through his papers. We were to become very accustomed to this very strange behaviour, and, as the days went on, I honestly think that he thought of himself as part of the legal team. He looked so unaffected and calm about his part in this, *his* trial. It only reinforced what I already knew.

Waiting for the trial to start, I got a sense of what it must feel like to be drowning. Our life up until Rachel's murder was flashing through my head, and I could almost feel those carefree days as I tried to make sense of what had gone wrong, mourning the 'what ifs'. All I could do was wonder: why? Why this young couple, who had it all? Joe had a very good job, a beautiful wife who adored him, two beautiful children, a lovely home and more importantly the good health to enjoy it all. It all should have been so different, but it is a sad truth that some people just don't get it – they can't see that they have it all. As they say, the grass is always greener on the other side, and while the majority of us can recognize that, there will always be those out there that want more. Some people are never happy, and rather than feeling fulfilled with what they have, they find that familiarity breeds contempt. Such people can never recognize that the real problem lies within themselves. As I thought the same thoughts over and over again, I could not help but think what a waste it had all been. I became more and more despondent sitting there, until I felt as if my own heartbeat was smothering me. I had no sense of time passing, as it all felt so unreal.

At last, shortly after midday, once the jury had been appointed and sworn in, the court rose as the Trial Justice, Barry White, entered the court. Next the jury appeared, and, as they filed into their seats, I remember praying to myself, *Please God, help them to reach an honest and firm decision when the time comes*. I was steadfast in my own belief and I prayed that they would see the truth for themselves.

Throughout the trial, I would try not to look directly at the jury. I cannot explain why, but I guess I was afraid they might think I was trying to influence them in some way, and I wanted them to come to their decision independently. I know now that my fears were unfounded and it was just one of the many worries you bring on yourself in a situation like that. From where I was sitting it was possible for me to see all twelve faces, and I know I would have glanced at them many times during the long days of the trial but I now find it hard to bring their faces to mind. I know the burden they must have felt following the details of the trial – so much depended upon them, and I was very aware that theirs was a very heavy responsibility. And so it began.

Even on the first day of the case, our nerves were tested to the limit. Just after we arrived back from a lunch break in the proceedings and were waiting for things to start up again, there seemed to be some confusion going on between the judge and the barristers. A potential juror alleged that he had been told by one of the jurors before she was sworn in that she thought Joe was guilty. As jurors, of course, are not permitted to speak about the trial while it is underway, and they are to remain impartial until the evidence is presented, this was a huge problem. It seemed at this point that the trial was on the verge of collapse, but the prosecution and defence came to an agreement that, if the said juror was let go, neither side would have any objections. That meant we now had only eleven jurors instead of twelve, and one less woman – we had understood that it was better for the prosecution to have more women on the jury, as the victim was a woman, so even though it was a minus for the prosecution, it was far better than having to start the whole process over again. Choosing a new jury would have meant another delay, so we were grateful that justice was done and it was allowed to continue.

To our total dismay, the trial was later threatened with collapse for a second time. I will never forget the feelings of panic and I wondered: how on earth are we going to cope? We learned that part of the Book of Evidence was discovered in the Jury Room. As the jury is only allowed to see the evidence that the legal teams feel will hold up in court, by law, they are never supposed to see the Book of Evidence, which contains all of the evidence collected in the case. Instead, the jury's role is to make their decision based only on the information presented to them in court, not on the

witness statements taken during the police investigation or the other evidence collected against the
accused. The legal teams decide what evidence can
hold up in court, and what parts of the evidence
will best help their case, so some of the information
contained in the Book of Evidence would never be
made known to the jury. No one ever explained
how these documents ended up in the wrong
place, but the fact that they had meant that the Jury
might be dismissed. If that happened, the whole
trial would likely have to be rescheduled and would
probably not take place until the following year.
When I heard that, I suddenly found it hard to
breathe. I have never prayed as hard, and I was
doing all I could to keep a grasp on what was going
on. Justice Barry White called in the jury and put
a question to them: 'Did any one of you read
anything in that Book of Evidence, any portion or
any statement?' And under oath, each jury member
shook their head and replied 'No.' 'I am obliged
to make this enquiry,' Justice White said. 'I am
not casting any dispersions.' He then asked both
the prosecution and defence if they had any
objections, and when both answered, 'No,' the trial
was allowed to continue. At this point, I was very
worried that Judge Barry White might be too hard
on the prosecution, but as the days went on I came

to understand that he was a very fair man, and while I did not agree with every decision he made, I gave thanks to God that we had got a just man to conduct the trial.

14. The Early Days of the Trial

After the shock of the Book of Evidence situation, we realized how close we had come to a mistrial, and it seemed to drain every last ounce of energy we had left. That feeling of total exhaustion stayed with us for the rest of the trial, as we knew that anything could happen and an overwhelming fear accompanied us to court each and every day after that. Between that fear and the anxiety of what would be revealed in court each day, the trial was a nightmare that is hard to put into words. I found the thought of going to the court every morning very hard, and yet it would not have occurred to me to stay away. Having to look at Joe O'Reilly day in, day out, as he sat there so completely unfazed about the situation he was in while we were in a vortex of emotions, made me so very angry. The tension of having to sit there in the same room with him, while we were so upset and devastated and at other times heartbroken at what we were hearing as the trial unfolded, at times got to be unbearable for us. Joe, on the other hand, sat there, calmly and confidently going through papers from his folder, making notes and holding conversations with any- body near by who was willing to talk to him. The most upsetting part was when he would comment and pass notes on what was happening in the trial to and occasionally talk with his legal team. At times like these, I kept on thinking of Rachel and how she had been so betrayed. This just seemed to me to be yet another betrayal, his casual, jovial mood during his own trial for her murder, and it was one I found particularly hard to take. I had no choice but to try to block Joe O'Reilly's very existence from my mind on those awful days, but it was an impossibility, and I found myself looking at him and trying to fathom how someone who looked so normal could be so evil. I can never again as long as I live look at him without seeing what really lies beneath his façade.

The simple goal of getting justice for Rachel gave each of us the courage and strength to go in each day and be there for her. Jim, Declan, Paul,

Anthony, Ann and I attended each day, and only someone who has experienced attending a trial in similar circumstances can have a clue what that takes to get through it all. Each evening we would return after a day spent in court and would not even have the energy to answer the phone. It took all of our strength to prepare for the next day's proceedings and get through the day. When I look back I honestly do not know how we survived that awful time and, once again, I remember Pat and Phyl from Victim Support who were there for us each day. They would chat and help to take our mind off the situation as much as they could. I realize now how much that support is needed and so generously given.

Acting on behalf of the State was Denis Vaughan Buckley, a very experienced Senior Counsel who during his distinguished career had worked on some of the biggest murder trials in Ireland. The second barrister for the prosecution was a young man called Dominick McGinn. Our family had met them before the trial, and I had the utmost confidence in them. We were very lucky to have them on our side, and we were happy that things rested in their very capable hands. Vaughan Buckley opened the trial by explaining to the jury that the case was almost completely based on circumstantial evidence, but it was the prosecution's view that there was ample evidence to prove beyond reasonable doubt that Joe O'Reilly did indeed have a motive and the opportunity to murder his wife. The issue before them was whether Joe O'Reilly had in fact carried out the deed. He spoke for some time, outlining facts of the case and the evidence that the jury would hear. You could hear a pin drop as everyone in the small crowded courtroom hung on to his every word. Throughout the case, as a family, we found it very distressing to have to sit in public and listen to the very detailed accounts of some of the injuries that our daughter had received. Horrendous though it was to listen to, I could not help but think that it was nowhere near as bad as having actually seen what had been done to her.

We also heard the contents of the letter that Joe had written and placed in Rachel's coffin. It was dated four days after her murder, 8 October 2004; it read:

Rachel, I love you so very, very much. I cannot think what I will ever do without you and I don't want to think. You are the best thing that ever happened to me and you will never be replaced. This is the hardest letter I've ever had to write for reasons only we know. Rachel, forgive me. Two words, one sentence but I will say them forever. I look at our eldest child and I see you and hear you and smell you. I remember you. You have touched the lives of so many and made us better people. You made me laugh, you always did. Everyone loves you now and they always will. You were a smoker. You kept that quiet fair play to you. I am sorry about your Mum finding out about Theresa, Thomas and co. but please don't blame me, it wasn't my fault. I miss you so much Rachie. Please, please remember that. You went away from this world so very young. The world will remember how beautiful you were. Like Peter Pan you will never grow old. Softball misses you, hockey is after naming a trophy after you. Everyone misses your mad personality and can do attitude. Ian is heartbroken, your family, my family, everybody. Please look out for Jackie, your family and our children. I need you as well. Happy 31st birthday. You're no doubt having the best wine, the best coffee, the best ciggies. Rachel, I love you and I miss you and I will mourn you forever.

XXX

Your hubby wubby Jofes.

Love you Mammy,
Your loving children XXX

While Dominick McGinn read the letter aloud, Joe sat on the bench giving the performance of his life. He had a look on his face which I had seen before, and he could switch from one Joe to the other, bringing out whichever one was called for. Now, he played to perfection the part of the grieving husband and kept up his image – he even did the tears in the courtroom. Joe could feign emotion he was incapable of feeling, just like when he had suggested himself when he asked a journalist if he should cry for an interview. I had grown to know what to expect from him, but it was still one of the hardest parts for me, as I knew he was guilty. He had ensured that I saw firsthand what he had done to the wife he was now professing to love and miss so much. When I saw through his mask, I could see the hatred and loathing that motivated him. Some people thought that he felt some kind of remorse, but it was just another ploy he had orchestrated so carefully. The reality of what those little children have lost is heartbreaking, and I wonder how Joe could even look at them, knowing what he had done.

The prosecution then began the slow process of calling the witnesses. One of the first witnesses was John Doyle, a meteorologist. I was puzzled as to how his expert explanation of the weather conditions on the day of the murder being sunny and dry would be relevant. Next to give evidence was Eddie Kirk, the headmaster of the school that Rachel's eldest had been attending at the time of her death. He had been very supportive and helpful to the devastated little child in his care, which meant a great deal to us. More importantly, Mr Kirk testified that, when Joe came to collect the child from school at lunchtime on the day of the murder, his demeanour was calm and collected, not frantic as one might expect a man whose wife was missing to be.

It wasn't until the next morning that I was informed that I was to give evidence in court that day. I did not know what to expect. I tried to stay focused, but I was feeling very nervous. I was dreading sitting up there and going over the whole thing again, but I told myself that I just had to answer any questions I was asked with the truth. I had nothing to be nervous about, because the only one trying to cover up what really happened was Joe. That thought calmed me, and I was able to answer with confidence.

After I had given my evidence about what had happened on 4 October, I stepped down with the strange feeling of not having said enough to give the real picture of what had actually happened. The truth is that there are no words to describe what I had witnessed that day or how it felt, but I will always feel that I should have explained it better.

It was not until after both Jim and I had given our evidence that I realized we would no longer be able to sit in court to hear the next witnesses. This was because the judge had advised that some evidence in the Book of Evidence could be prejudicial to people who might be called again as witnesses, and, as such, it would require legal argument. I did not understand how a trial worked regarding the process of legal argument, but apparently all possibly contentious evidence was first heard in the absence of a jury, and then a process of legal argument began between the prosecution and defence to establish what part of the evidence was probative to the prosecution. During this time, neither the jury nor the witnesses who had already spoken could be present. We could not be there because we could not risk being influenced by the testimony of other people and the evidence that they gave, in case we had to be called again. That part was very hard, because naturally we didn't want to miss anything that was important to the trial. We sat in the Round Room, an area directly under the dome of the Four Courts, for each of those four days. Meanwhile, inside Court 2, Ann and Anthony were accompanied by my sister, Susan, and her husband, Kevin. Declan and Paul, who were potential witnesses, also sat out with us.

Even if we couldn't hear what was going on, we were happier to be in the building, and during the few days that we were sitting in the Round Room, we were able to meet some of the witnesses. One of them was a priest, an elderly man called Father Stephen Redmond. By chance, he had been out with a friend in the vicinity of The Naul on the day of Rachel's murder. I had met him outside Rachel's house on that awful day. He told me that, as they were driving, they happened to take a wrong turn. When they got as far as Rachel's house, they noticed an ambulance and all the activity outside and stopped to see if they could be of any assistance. He was allowed in to see Rachel and his gentleness and compassion on that day will always stay with us. It was strange that he should have been in that spot at that time, and I took his presence as another indication of God's hand in our lives.

We did not see the first witnesses who gave evidence, including Helen, who runs the crèche, and several of the young mums who would have seen Rachel in the last hour of her life. Nor did I hear the milkman's evidence, but I hope I will get to meet him some day. He should know that Rachel was very fond of their chats, and appreciated his friendliness. It goes to show you how our inter-actions with the people we meet in our everyday lives can have an impact on those around us. His was a friendly hand held out to her, and Rachel had told me how much she appreciated it. Another such case was James McNally, a farmer who owns land directly across the road from Lambay View. He used to invite Rachel up so that the children could see his cows, which they loved. I had never met James before Rachel died, but I know that he was another friendly face who helped her to feel at home in The Naul.

I missed Jim's, Anthony's, Paul's and my daughter-in-law Denise's testimony while we were still out in the Round Room. I would have liked to have seen Joe's face as the boy whom he had befriended now stood before him in the witness box. Anthony had looked up to Joe so much, and he had so enjoyed sharing his interest in films with his brother-in-law. They had spent a good amount of time together over the years, and he had accom-panied Joe on many trips to the cinema. Anthony, too, had been taken in by Joe, and was devastated when he learned what Joe had done to his sister and her children. I will never forget the effect it had on him; he will never get over it, but none of that had any effect on Joe. The thought that he could betray the friendship of a younger man who admired him, his brother-in-law, and have absolutely no compunction about doing so just shows Joe to be the heartless monster he really is, and how he had no respect whatsoever for our family. I would not expect anything different from him, and his motivations are simply beyond understanding.

The ripples of destruction that Joe sent into the lives of Rachel's loved ones are endless. Joe made sure that Jackie would suffer the sadness of her best friend's loss every year on her birthday. We missed Jackie's testimony about what happened on her birthday, Monday 4 October 2004, as Jim and I were still in the Round Room. Jackie was the one who had the most insight into how things really were in Rachel's marriage, as Rachel trusted Jackie and would have confided in her. She really loved Rachel, and the feeling was certainly mutual. Jackie could also attest to how Joe tried to manipulate her that day to make out he did not commit the murder. She wasn't alone in that, because Joe tried to manipulate anybody he thought might give him an alibi for the relevant few hours, including another young woman who went out of her way to help him with the kids after Rachel's death. Naomi Gargan was a young mum with a child in the same crèche as Rachel's youngest. She felt very sorry for Joe and offered to help him in any way she could. She started to collect and mind the youngest child in her home until Joe could come. For her trouble, Joe tried to weave her into his web of lies. When he went to her house to collect the child, he would explain that 'they' were following him and reading his text messages, and that he was going to be arrested and held for questioning. He said that rumours were going around that he was having an affair, and that she could be the one he was having an affair with. He told her not to be surprised if she was brought in for questioning. Naomi was finding out for herself that things were not how she first imagined with Joe. His behaviour was getting more and more bizarre, both in the comments he made to her and the way he came across. It seemed like Joe was letting everyone know that it wasn't just him who was under suspicion; he wanted the people around him to know that they could be next. Naomi became very afraid of him and stopped having any contact with him.

Back at Court Number 2, many more of Rachel's friends, members of the Fire Brigade who had arrived in the ambulance and many more passed through the witness box to give their evidence, and it was a great help for us to see all of the people who had come forward to do their part in getting justice for Rachel. I do think sometimes of all of those who could have made such a positive difference from the very start and saved an awful lot of heartache and unnecessary work for the Gardaí. Sometimes it takes extraordinary courage to stand up and come forward, and, though it may not always be easy, we are all capable of trying to make this a better world for our children to inherit.

15. Living in Dread of the Next Awful Revelation

Jim and I had given our evidence during the process of legal argument, and, once it was complete, we could again take our places on that uncomfortable wooden bench. We were there for every second of the trial after that. The police could not tell us very much, but they did try to prepare us as much as they could, warning that there would be traumatic days ahead. As each day of the trial slowly passed, we grew to dread what revelations might come to light as the true Joe O'Reilly began to appear. Some particularly distressing evidence was put forward by the prosecution, only to be deemed inadmissible by Justice White, which was very hard on us and still seems very unfair. It felt as if the screws were being turned, and the pain went from bad to worse. We endured hour after hour of excruciating testimony that showed us a true picture of what Rachel had to live with every day.

The physical evidence was more difficult for us again. Dr Diane Daly, the forensic scientist on the case, was able to determine how Rachel had met her violent end by studying the pattern of the blood splatter at the scene of the murder. That very graphic description of what Rachel was forced to endure before she finally died will never leave us. Once more I wished earnestly that Joe O'Reilly would be confronted with the horror of what he had done before he closed his eyes each night.

Dr Daly revealed that blood had been found on the door of the washing machine that forensics had removed from the utility room. The blood did not belong to Joe, but rather to Rachel's half-brother Thomas, who had cut his hand with a saw when he was helping them to build the decking out the back garden in August 2004, just a few weeks before the murder. While he was attending his wound, some blood dripped on to the door of the washing machine. Rachel told him she would look after it, but obviously she did not get around to it. Even though the only reason Thomas had been there was to do work around the house for Joe, it did not stop Joe from casting suspicion on him once the trial began. Again, it just shows how despicable and vindictive Joe O'Reilly really is, as it didn't even matter to him that Thomas was out doing the work Joe should have been doing himself. Joe's defence put Thomas through a terrible grilling about his alibi on the morning of the murder, and it was an awful ordeal for him to be put through.

The State Pathologist, Dr Marie Cassidy, then took the stand. She told the hushed court that, from her examinations of Rachel's body, it appeared that Rachel had tried to defend herself as she was being beaten so brutally. She testified that she may have lain dying for hours. Dr Cassidy explained in detail how Rachel was struck a number of times on the head, fracturing her skull, but that these injuries probably did not kill her instantly as they were inflicted by a blunt object. It was such a savage beating that Dr Cassidy was unable to say how many blows Rachel had received. There were eight lacerations to her head, but determining the exact number of blows would depend on what weapon was used, and they could not find the murder weapon. She explained that the injuries to her forehead indicated that Rachel could have been standing upright when the first blow was struck – a blow that did not kill her, but could have caused concussion. Dr Cassidy went on to explain in detail the rest of the horrific injuries inflicted on our daughter as she lay dying on the ground. While she was unconscious, Rachel inhaled blood, and a fracture to the right side of the back of her skull was consistent with bleeding in, and damage to, the brain. Rachel also had extensive bruising to the right side of her face. Even as I write it all down now, I wonder how I will ever get that picture out of my mind. I fear I never will.

A very good friend of both Rachel and Joe, Alan Boyle, who had been one of the groomsmen at their wedding, gave evidence at the trial during legal argument. Early on in the investigation, he had given a statement to the Gardaí about how Joe re-enacted the murder for him, just a couple of days after it had happened. When Alan first heard of Rachel's murder, he was very shocked and went out to the house in Baldarragh to see Joe and give him his support, but when he got there, he was very confused at Joe's behaviour. Joe was so cool and matter-of-fact about the situation that it did not seem right to Alan. Joe offered to do 'The Tour', as it was later to become known, bringing Alan down to the bedroom, pointing out the blood splatters and offering his view on how the murder had been committed. He had done the same for Alan as he had done for us, once again going into detail, kneeling down to show how the blows had been made. Joe told Alan that he believed the killer had waited in the bedroom for Rachel.

The two men returned to the kitchen and were going through the possibilities of who could have done it. I suppose that Alan was getting the feeling by this point that he was missing something, and he asked Joe if it was possible that Rachel could have been having an affair. Whatever Alan was thinking at this stage, he definitely was not prepared for Joe's reaction: 'I couldn't give a fuck what Rachel had,' said Joe. It was the cold and angry way in which Joe said it that shocked Alan the most – after all, Joe's wife had just been killed. Alan told Joe that all the Gardaí had at that point in time was circumstantial evidence, but that if they were to get more hard evidence, he would have difficulty believing that Joe was innocent. Alan told the court Joe replied, 'When you stop believing me, let me know.' Alan made several attempts to contact Joe afterwards, but Joe never returned his calls. He then rang Joe's mother's house and left messages, saying that he was around if Joe wanted to go for a pint, but there was still no word. He never had any contact with his friend Alan after this.

Jackie, Rachel's friend, had also given evidence

about a very strange conversation that she had with Joe. He told her that he lay down in the spot where Rachel had died, and that Rachel had come to him in a dream, but that their conversation ended abruptly when Joe's sister, Anne, came into the room. Jackie found it disturbing, but Joe continued the story the next time he met Jackie two days later in the house in Baldarragh. Jackie was standing in the bedroom where the murder had occurred, and Joe was standing close to her in the hallway. Joe continued the story where he had left off, telling Jackie that, in the dream, Rachel had got two blows to the head, and when the killer heard her gurgling and choking on her blood, they went back and whacked her on the head. He told Jackie that they had held Rachel down – that's why there was so much blood splattered around. Joe explained that the dream was Rachel's way of letting him know what happened from beyond the grave. Joe told Jackie that he had given information to the Gardaí about two missing brown towels and a dumbbell which he said was missing from his room. Joe repeated to Jackie that he believed it was somebody Rachel trusted and that whoever it was had known exactly what they were doing. He even went so far as to say that the area behind the ear was the correct place to hit someone if you want to kill them and he added someone with military training would know this. Jackie was horrified, and it turned out that she wasn't the only one of Rachel's friends who heard the same explanation from Joe.

Joe told another of Rachel's friends, Celine Keogh, that Rachel had appeared to him in a dream. He claimed that in the dream, Rachel kept directing him to the spare bedroom next to their bedroom and saying, 'Think, Joe.' He said that it came to him that it was something to do with this room, which was where he kept his weights, and he understood that Rachel was telling him that one of the weights was the murder weapon. Joe had also told me a dream story almost identical to the one he told Celine and many of Rachel's friends.

Fidelma Geraghty was one of the locals in The Naul with whom Rachel had made friends. They used to go for walks together, and Fidelma would visit Rachel on Tuesday nights when Joe wasn't there. We now know that Joe had started to spend Tuesday nights with his mistress; once, it had been his night out with Rachel. Fidelma gave evidence during the trial that, after Rachel's murder, Joe had offered to give her 'The Tour'. When she declined, he tried to convince her by saying that a lot of people found it peaceful – clearly just another indication of his state of mind. Reluctantly, Fidelma agreed. Joe could not seem to help himself and kept telling people how Rachel had met her death, going over and over the whole scene, time after time. While she was there, Joe questioned her about the CCTV cameras up at Murphy's Quarry, probably assuming that, as Fidelma was well up on what went on in the area, she would be a good person to ask. He wanted to know how long they had been there, how good they were, whether she knew what type of camera they were, why they were pointing down at his house, and if it was possible to get the number of a registration plate from them. He told her that there had been newspaper reports that the Gardaí had obtained footage from the CCTV cameras, and he wanted to know more about them. Joe seemed very concerned and also questioned my son Paul about the presence of the cameras up at the quarry, again asking how long they had been there. He said that he had often walked around the quarry with the two children, and he had never seen them. Joe told Paul that, if he had been aware of them, he would have objected to them being there. Paul was surprised to hear how he felt and told him that, if he were in Joe's position, he would have been glad to find out that they were there, considering that they could bring new, helpful evidence to the case.

Another mutual friend of Joe and Rachel's, Fiona Slevin, gave evidence that Joe told her the Gardaí were looking for the murder weapon in the wrong place. 'I don't know why they're searching in the fields, it's in the water,' he told her. When he saw Fiona's face and realized what he had said, he added, 'If I had done it, that's where it would be, because there's water all around and it would get rid of DNA and all of that sort of stuff.' Fiona could not believe what she was hearing. Joe's remarks that day were another piece of the jigsaw that was coming together to form a damning picture before our very eyes.

James McNally, Rachel's neighbour, told the court that he had been unable to go to Rachel's funeral due to work commitments, so, when he met Joe on Friday 15 October, he told him he was sorry he could not attend the funeral and sympathized with him on his loss. Joe asked him if he had seen anything the morning of the murder, and James told him that he and his son had passed a red car on the road. Joe told James that the Gardaí had traced the car, and that it was a red Mercedes. James told the courtroom emphatically that, in his opinion, it was a red Ford Escort. A week or two later, James stopped to talk to Joe again, and, during the course of the conversation, asked Joe who he thought did it. Joe answered by saying, 'We are all suspects. You are a suspect, I am a suspect . . .' James smiled and said, 'I know where I was.'

Many of the employees from Viacom were called upon to give evidence, and not one of them was able to give Joe an alibi – with the exception of Derek Quearney, whose testimony I'll describe later. The managing director of Viacom, Philip Brown, recounted in court a conversation he had with Joe while they were having lunch at the Shelbourne Hotel on 26 October. Mr Brown told the court his conversation with Joe remained 'fairly' clear in his mind. Joe told him that he had one or two suspicions about who murdered Rachel, and that it may have been a man from NTL who he had asked to install an alarm, and that he wanted the police to question the man. He also said that he was convinced that the killer knew Rachel. At another point in the conversation, Joe said that the crime scene was very messy, that there was a lot of blood and that he had embraced Rachel, and as a result, he was conscious that he may have contaminated the evidence. Joe also pointed the finger at their next-door neighbours, Kevin and Maura Moore, making out that they might have a grudge against Rachel in connection with a boundary at the end of their garden. Philip Brown was not to know that there was never any ill feeling between Rachel and the Moores. Rachel had mentioned something to me at the time about the boundary, but it certainly did not cause conflict between her and her neighbours. Joe had clearly tried to throw suspicion on anyone he could think of who had any contact with Rachel whatsoever.

16. Learning the Shattering Truth about Rachel's Marriage

As time passed, it became clear that Joe's efforts to cast doubts on others were no use, thanks to impressive technology that is advancing so fast. Technology was in a way a key witness of this trial, and I am so thankful that Joe's careful plans did not allow for advances in technology. In his arrogance, he still thought that he could get away with it, and that he had left no tracks behind him.

The testimony of Detective Garda Sean Fitzpatrick was extremely important in proving Joe to be the murderer he is. Detective Fitzpatrick had spent weeks collecting and analysing 119 separate pieces of CCTV footage obtained by the Gardaí as part of their investigation. The CCTV images were collected from numerous locations around North

Dublin and the area surrounding Joe's workplace in Bluebell, as well as the front reception area. Garda Fitzpatrick produced a map marked with sightings of vehicles similar to Joe's navy blue Fiat estate car, which was displayed on two large plasma screens on the walls either side of the judge's bench. Step by step the jury was shown by Garda Fitzpatrick the journey that Gardaí believe Joe made that morning. It showed where he left his workplace, his route out to the house in Baldarragh and, finally, the journey back in to the north of the city. Joe's car is not a very common model, which made the many pictures captured on CCTV all the more important. Sightings of the car correlated exactly to the timing and location of signals registered by each telephone mast from his mobile phone as he made that fateful journey, a trip which took place at the time that Joe claimed he was at the Broadstone bus depot inspecting the advertisements on buses.

The footage taken from the reception area of Joe's workplace in Bluebell clearly showed that at 08.07 a.m. Joe left the premises. Footage from another camera showed a car similar to Joe's leaving the industrial estate at 08.12 a.m. Detective Fitzpatrick described several sightings of a similar car along the route to his home, but the sighting that chilled me to the bone was that of Rachel's

Renault Scenic passing the quarry at 09.03 a.m. She would have been making her last journey to school with her two children. Detective Fitzpatrick went on to give evidence of a navy-blue estate car caught on CCTV passing the entrance to the quarry at 09.10.32 a.m., just seven minutes after Rachel had left, heading in the direction of his house. Joe had timed it perfectly.

A vehicle was seen heading in the direction of the O'Reilly household at 09.41.29 a.m., which the detective believed to be Rachel's Renault Scenic. Listening to him describe her driving along, unaware of what was to come, conjured up such real and devastating images that I wonder how we could have sat through it. At 09.59.22 a.m., just eighteen minutes later, the detective observed what he believed to be Joe's navy Fiat Marea pass the entrance of the quarry, driving away from the house and back towards the city. Eighteen minutes was all it took for Joe to carry out the carefully planned execution. It was obvious that a lot of thought and preparation had gone into this completely premeditated killing.

One of many tasks that Detective Garda Jim McGovern had to complete was a reconstruction of the journey that Gardaí believe Joe made that morning. Detective McGovern set out at the same time that Joe did, bringing his own mobile phone with him. The supporting evidence from this reconstruction showed that Detective McGovern's phone registered at the same masts that Joe's had, and at almost identical times, all of which reinforced the initial technological evidence from Detective Fitzpatrick's mapped journey made with the CCTV imagery stills. The Gardaí had sent the CCTV footage to the UK, to Andrew Laws, a CCTV imagery expert. He studied and analysed all of the images and presented his findings to the court. He told the court that, having done the analysis, he could not rule out the possibility that a car seen at Murphy's Quarry on the day and at the time of Rachel's murder was Joe's, and therefore he would class the evidence as giving 'moderate support' to this theory, as it was possible that the car in question was the same make and model as Joe's. He was also of the opinion that a car seen near Blake's Cross, eight kilometres south of Rachel's house, was the same make and model as Joe's car.

Sitting there listening to evidence and knowing full well what had actually happened within these time frames brought me right back to the carnage I had walked in on that terrible day. Frame by frame, the terrible images kept coming into my head, and I could picture Joe driving out on his journey to the house. How could he possibly carry out the horrendous act he had planned? How, when the mother of his two children entered the house, having just kissed them goodbye, could he not show her some mercy? How could he end Rachel's life so brutally and savagely? I could not help but wonder what he was actually thinking as he was driving along.

The full extent of Joe's affair with Nikki Pelley was key to the development of the trial, and through her cross-examination, the court learned a great deal more about Joe's true nature and ability to deceive. It emerged during the trial that Joe had told Nikki, when she was asked about the affair, not to say that it was a relationship, but to do as he had done and insist that it was just a sexual affair. The judge had warned her to tell the truth while she was under oath, and finally she answered the question put to her by the prosecution as to why Joe would advise her to lie about their relationship. When pressed, she told the court that Joe told her that, if she told the truth, it would look like he had a motive to kill Rachel.

The morning that we were informed that Nikki Pelley was to give evidence that day, we also learned

Rachel, Joe and their first baby in the Rotunda in March 2000. She had a difficult pregnancy and was very sick the whole time. It really was unusually bad, and we did all we could to help. But when the baby was born, it had truly all been worthwhile. The baby was beautiful, and looked so much like Rachel herself.

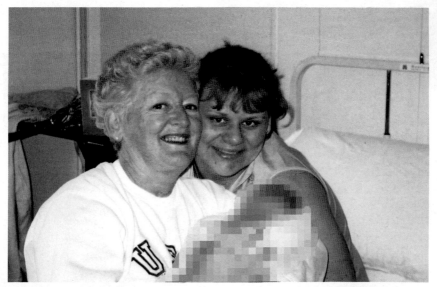

Here I am with Rachel and her baby in the Rotunda, celebrating the arrival of our first grandchild within hours of the birth.

Left: Rachel, Joe and their first baby at the christening party in May 2000.

Above: Two proud parents on their first-born's first birthday in March 2001.

Below: The new mother having a nap with her baby

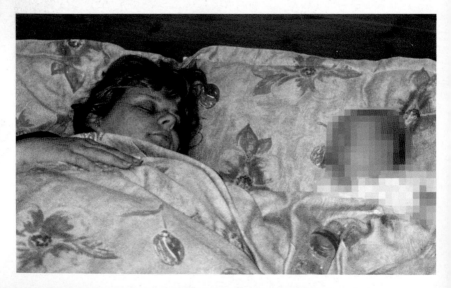

Christmas 2000 and our annual family gathering had grown again. My daughter-in-law Denise and Paul's fiancé, also Denise, are to the left of the picture and our first grandchild was adored by all of us.

By the end of 2001 Rachel had given birth to her second baby and the picture shows the two children with their proud mother, aunt and grandparents after the second child's christening in January 2002.

Left: Joe, Rachel and Ann at our son Paul and Denise's wedding in Rome in August 2002. When I look back at the pictures of that dinner, I am amazed that I did not notice the sullen look on Joe's face and how Rachel did not seem to have the same sparkle in her eyes.

Below: The annual family get-together on Christmas Day 2002. Rachel is just behind me. The following Christmas Day, her last one, Joe launched a major attack on her in front of me, supposedly about not inviting us out to them for a meal. I tried to defuse things but her eyes filled with tears and she rushed the children out the door and didn't wait for the customary photographs.

Left: A portrait of Rachel with her two children in early 2003. My greatest wish in life is that they will grow up in the knowledge of how much she loved them and that they were her reason for living. She was so looking forward to seeing them grow up. She had two boxes at home, their 'Treasure Chests', into which she put keepsakes from time to time. She intended to continue until it was time for them to leave home, and then she was going to give each of them their own box.

Below: This family portrait was done in early 2004. It is heartbreaking to think that behind this image of a normal young family Rachel was being undermined and criticized at every turn.

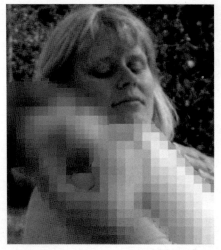

Summer 2003. Rachel holding her sleepy youngest child in her new garden in The Naul.

2004. Rachel playing softball. In April her team got into *The Guinness Book of Records* for holding the world's longest softball game.

Rachel loved doing things with the children and took them everywhere with her. Here they are in high spirits at a family day in Ardgillan Park in Skerries only a few weeks before she died.

One of our favourite pictures of Rachel – aged about twenty and with that beautiful smile.

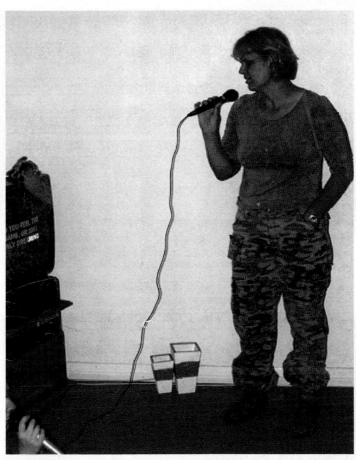

Rachel's last picture – singing karaoke in her friend Celine's house on
Friday 1 October 2004, just three days before her death. She is singing
The Bangles' song 'Eternal Flame'.

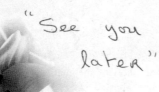

The card on the flowers Joe got
for his wife's funeral said it all: 'See
you later, Joe.' Not another word,
just that stark message amid the
outpouring of compassion on cards
from strangers. Yet her husband's
message did not use her name and
there was no mention of love.

The family arriving at the court the day of the verdict on the 21 July 2007. From left: me, Declan and his wife, Denise, Ann, Jim, Anthony and Paul.

The scene outside the court after we came out following the guilty verdict. Though our fight was not yet over, because Joe O'Reilly appealed the verdict, at least he had finally been exposed and named for what he was: a murderer. Thank God his appeal was unsuccessful and after the court's decision in March this year (2009) we could finally rejoice in the knowledge that justice had been upheld. Rachel could now rest peacefully.

that she had been called as a witness for the prosecution. I felt sort of sorry for her, because I assumed that she was going to answer the questions that would be put to her truthfully, and I knew it would not be easy for her. But despite her having promised to answer truthfully, and regardless of her previous statements to Gardaí, once she was in the witness box, her testimony did not go as we had expected. She answered again and again that she could not remember, to the point that the judge reminded her of her duty to tell the truth while under oath. My pity for Nikki Pelley evaporated as I listened to her, but as Vaughan Buckley, SC, went through the emails, text messages and Joe's talk of love for Nikki, I could not help but wonder if she couldn't see that Rachel had once heard the very same things from Joe. Did she not ask herself if, some day, she would be in the same position that Rachel had found herself in once Joe tired of her and moved on? Did she think that Joe was somehow incapable of speaking her name with the same awful hatred he had shown for Rachel, that somehow she could never be subjected to the vile descriptions and lies she so readily accepted of Rachel? Did she not wonder if, some day, she might be the next victim of the same demented reasoning that allowed Joe to kill Rachel, though

I sincerely hope he never again gets the opportunity to hurt anybody. All of these thoughts raced through my mind as I tried to come to terms with what we were hearing.

The email evidence which was so important to the case was provided by the headquarters of the company Joe was working for, Viacom. Fortunately, Joe thought that he had deleted all the emails entirely, but a computer network engineer from Viacom, Roy Montgomery, told the court that he had been instructed by the Gardaí to copy any information from Joe's email account, which was connected to the company's server, on to a CD. This record contained all of the emails sent and received by Joe, and it had been handed over to the Gardaí during the investigation.

As difficult as the introduction of the email evidence was for each of us, we were very grateful that modern technology could give us concrete proof of what we already knew. The evidence extended beyond details of Joe's affair – it was like looking at a complete catalogue of events leading up to Rachel's brutal murder. Nothing could have prepared us for the venom and hatred shown towards Rachel, and it showed the world the true extent of the psychological abuse in Rachel and

Joe's home. No amount of manipulation could eradicate the proof of what they had said, and we could thank the IT experts involved in the case for their help in making technology testify for Rachel. We were shocked when Joe's lies began to unravel, and the truth emerged, and my heart broke for her as the most private details of her life were exposed and put under public scrutiny. Though Rachel had no chance to defend her good name, at least the public could get an insight into how things had been turned against her in her own home. The following transcripts were read aloud in Court Number 2.

From: Anne O'Reilly
Sent: June 9, 2004 10.16am
To: Joe O'Reilly
Subject:

Hi ya,

I'm just asking you know how you got on yesterday? How are you? Concerned Banana!

Wanted to leave you alone yesterday to get your head together but trust me I held back on calling or mailing you.

Let me know how things are and if you need anything.

From: Joe O'Reilly
Sent: June 9, 2004 10.41am
To: Anne O'Reilly
Subject:

Hi ya Anne,

In a nutshell, it was a big steaming pile of shite. They told us BOTH, that shouting at the kids was okay, 'sure we all do it'. Hitting kids is okay in the eyes of the law, as again, 'we all do it.' They never come out and visit the homes of kids reported as being abused unless the allegation is of a sexual nature or after SEVERAL cases of non-accidental hospitalisations. Could it have gone any worse????? YES!!!

Rachel is a 'good mother' because she admits to having problems dealing with the kids and confessed to shouting at them on a daily basis. There is some Mickey Mouse course run once a year, to help parents cope with 'difficult kids' and 'parenting difficulties,' and Rachel has volunteered to go on one. She was also playing the 'home help' card but didn't get anywhere. The best I got was a commitment to getting the district nurse to pay a visit, as the youngest is due a developmental check-up. Should have got it last year, but in Rachel's words 'you know yourself, with the house move and so on, it's easy to forget these things.' Anyway, I gave them the go-ahead to drop out whenever they want to see the kids. Hopefully the DN will see her at her 'best' or else the state of the house that the lazy c**t leaves it in etc . . .

Positives? Very few. At least it's on the record that I don't need to attend the course, I've no issues in dealing with the kids, and the complaint had nothing to do with me. To answer your question as to how I am. Well, to be honest, I wasn't expecting much, as you were no doubt aware so I wasn't too shocked with the apathy displayed by our wonderful child protection people. That said, I think matters may get worse as she told me in the car park that 'I knew you were over-reacting going on to me about shouting at the kids. Did you hear them? Everybody does it, and I am a good mother.'

Instead of giving her a slap on the wrist, it appears that they've forgiven her and patted her on the back for a job well done. Did you get to talk to Derek by the way? Had to physically restrain him on Saturday night, not good. He's too much of a hot-head, but that said, you really couldn't blame him, the youngest was 'reefed' up by the arm and dragged to bed, and she nearly tore the eldest's ears off putting on the PJs. As usual, I had a right go at her, but as usual, by that stage the damage is already done. Shouldn't really complain though, she is a 'Wonderful Mother' in the eyes of the state.

Joe

PS Interesting choice of terminology used by the social worker, everything was Rachel is the main care giver and I was the secondary care giver. I'm already 'Mr. Weekend Custody' in the eyes of the state. Doesn't bode too well does it? Oh, nearly forgot, the case is now closed to their satisfaction.

From: Anne O'Reilly
Sent: June 9, 2004 11.01am
To: Joe O'Reilly
Subject:

Well at least you get the DN coming out on unexpected visits
that cant be too bad really. Dan was talking to her yesterday
and she told him she now counts to 10 and examines the
situation with the kids, so let's hope something good even if
it's little will come of this.

So your going out for a meal on Friday night with her, should
be good fun all nice and romantic (not) try again to talk to her
about her lack of motherly instincts, have you told her she's
none? Does she admit to it. Try a bit harder to talk to her
about it, tell her everything, be open and honest I know I'd
keep on trying constantly I wouldn't give her ears a break
from the subject, otherwise she's just going to keep on liven
in cloud cookoo land.

Did Derek say anything to Rachel about her man handling
the kids? Ma was very worried about yesterday if you get a
minute could you ring her put her mind to rest. I went straight
into Ma's yesterday to see what the story was and she was
saying that Rachel came in was all over the youngest and
just blanked the other (fooking bitch) that hurt Ma she
wanted so much to say something but didn't, anyway Rachel
stayed for chips, egg and bread and was very calm and happy
so Ma was left thinking . . .

Call her she's our Mammy and does really worry about us :)

So do I still have to be on my best around Rachel keeping my mouth shut? If I see her hit or man handle the kids can I speak up?

From: Joe O'Reilly
Sent: June 9, 2004 3.42pm
To: Anne O'Reilly
Subject:

So, she now counts to ten eh? Believe that and you're not my sister!!! Where the hell did you hear I was going for a night out with that c**t???? A meal? I'd rather choke. Absolutely no way, never, not happening. To quote your goodself Anne, never look back, only look forward, eh? Just to drill the point home, Me + Rachel + Marriage = Over!!! I keep telling her, straight as you like, exactly what I think of her motherly instincts. She's under no illusions there. Do I tell her at every hands turn? Yes, in fact, to be even a little fair, I'm very aware that I'm over-critical at times, although I don't feel too guilty about it to be honest, as she repulses me. Derek didn't say anything, I wouldn't let him. Bad enough I have to bite my tongue and restrain myself, don't need him losing it. Not for her sake, but the kids wouldn't like seeing their mother abused by their uncle Derek, and I don't want his halo around them diminished in any way (you're getting competition

Anne!!). That's where you need to be careful, when Ma reported the incident, that brought about yesterday's farce, it very nearly came out as to who did the reporting!!! You're prime suspect number one, you know it. By all means, drag her fat ass outside and kick it into the middle of next week, but not in front of the kids, and don't leave any marks that can and will be used against you in a court of law . . .

As I've said repeatedly, there is no talking to her. She does not listen. Mind you there is a lot of that about . . . I told you and I told Ma this would amount to nothing, and you BOTH knew better than me and went through the usual series of questions. I'm not having a go Anne, but it really wound me up last time as I go through every single angle I can with the kids before I make a move. Yesterday proved yet again, injustices that exist in this country. As a mother, you can shout and scream and smack almost as much as you want, once you admit to having a bit of a problem and then volunteer to a lip service parents course.

Maybe now, you'll both listen to what I have to say and not go about with your heads in the sand. Being a father in this country, no matter how good, will land you with weekend visitations and not much else. You know of one case where full custody was given, that's great and good for him. I know of dozens where it went the other way. Yesterday was my 1st personal indication of how much I WILL lose if I don't try different angles. After all, I'm only the secondary care giver.

I do appreciate your support; and I know the kids mean the world to you, they are my life and I am nothing without them. The youngest was the one singled out as the child whom the concerns were about. More bad news for the eldest as proved yesterday, in your own words and observations. Anne, there is only so much crap that kid can deal with, and my patients are running on empty. YOU saw 1st hand the number she did before, I'D rather die than see the kid go through that again, END OF STORY. Be as good as you can around Rachel for now, but tell me EVERYTHING you see, do not hold back. If you see her being excessive, then step in. I want to know as much as possible, and I can't be there all the time.

Anne, you're my sister, my blood, she's not. What you tell me will not be questioned. You have my carte blanche visitation rights to my house, and to my kids. In fact the more you're around, the better. Same with Dan, but I don't want him knowing too much. I plan on calling Ma later tonight. I know she's worried, but I couldn't call last night, as I didn't know she still had a visitor and her family. The Worlds Greatest Mum is out tonight, getting laid with a bit of luck, so I'll have time to talk to Ma properly when the kids are asleep.

I'll be home in Ma's on Friday with the kids so I'll see you then?

Thanks for the concern, sorry for the long email!!

Joe

From: Anne O'Reilly
Sent: June 9, 2004 4.00pm
To: Joe O'Reilly
Subject:

Your meal is prob a surprise well of course it is – she got Dan
to booked it last night for ye's then you's are staying in Ma's
but she asked me last week if she ever wanted to venture up
to Dunleer and cat out could she stay with me??? So she
knows the marriage is over then and it's a divorce what does
she say to that? Maybe that's why she's taken you out on
Friday. Say nothing . . .

I do get it now your fooked as a Father in this dump ask her to
move abroad, I really dunno how your going to get out of this
one.

So when are ye's filling for Legal Separation then? If ye want I
Kidnap you and the kids on Friday night before she has chance
to get hold of you – we could go on a trip in my car??/or you
could just go out with her and ignore her the whole night or
stare at sexy ladies.

In one of the emails to his sister, Joe spoke of his
frustration about the complaint to Child Protection
Services about Rachel and the children, laying out
in his own words how he went through every angle
of the situation before he made his move. This

was certainly the case when he created a world of lies about Rachel in the lead-up to her murder. It was distressing to hear the completely fictitious descriptions of Rachel's lack of mothering instincts, and how she was subjected to cruel criticism, day in and day out. This treatment must have eroded any confidence or joy she felt rearing her two beloved children, and it was now clear that Rachel's two little children were being taken from her a long time before she was beaten to death. I look back on the satisfaction and pure joy we felt as we reared our children, and I know all of that was taken from Rachel, which causes me the greatest pain in all of the injustice that she suffered. It is my heartfelt wish that she will be remembered for the good and loving human being she really was.

17. Technology Destroys Joe O'Reilly's Alibi

Even when evidence was produced to prove that Joe was lying about having been at the Broadstone bus depot, Derek Quearney's evidence was that they had been there at the same time throughout that Monday morning. Using the information of where their respective mobile phones were located throughout the morning, prosecution counsel put it to Quearney that his evidence, which supported Joe's alibi, was wrong. Quearney maintained that his recollection when he was questioned by Gardaí was that the times he had said Joe was with him at Broadstone were correct. When pushed on the matter he said that in an interview with the Gardaí he had conceded that he 'could have been wrong' about the times he remembered seeing Joe on the morning of the murder. Detective Fitzpatrick, who had already given evidence about how Joe's car was identified on CCTV, was called at this point to give evidence about how Derek Quearney's car had also been traced on its journey as it went in the direction of the Broadstone depot.

In his testimony, Quearney said that he had met Joe at the gym early that morning and had then spoken to him at the Viacom offices. He said that Joe had set off for the Broadstone depot to inspect the buses first, and he had followed around 9.30 a.m. When Quearney arrived, he said that he rang Joe and asked him where he was. He told the police that Joe said he was at the back of the pits. Quearney went on to explain that he got out of his car and told Joe that he would find him. He then reported to the foreman that he was from Viacom and was doing an inspection, something that they were obliged to do each time they arrived and before they started work. Importantly, although Joe claimed to have arrived earlier, and would have been very familiar with the procedure, he never made contact with the foreman, nor did anyone at the depot see Joe there. Regardless, Quearney claimed that he had met up with Joe between 09.50 and 10.00 a.m. (about the time that Joe was leaving his home in The Naul to head back to the

Broadstone) and they then split up to inspect buses separately. He said that he met Joe again at 10.30am, and they inspected more buses together before leaving to head back to the Viacom offices in Bluebell at about 11.00 a.m.

Joe, on the other hand, had told the detectives that, when he arrived at the Broadstone depot that morning, he saw a Viacom van, but not the driver, an employee called Damian Tully. He did claim to have seen Damian Tully's mobile phone on the front seat of the van. According to the roster for that day, Damian should have been in the Broadstone depot that morning, but, by another twist of fate, one of his colleagues called in sick, and Damian was sent to another job site instead. Luck did not seem to be on Joe's side that morning, for Damian's whereabouts were later proven when it was discovered that his van was clamped outside Pearse Street Garda Station at the time Joe had supposedly seen it at the Broadstone depot. Joe's plan had backfired yet again, as he had not allowed for Murphy's Law ruining his careful plan, and his lies were exposed.

During the investigation, the detectives found out from mobile phone records that Joe and Derek Quearney were not in the same place when they spoke to each other. When the Gardaí showed

Quearney the calls he made to Joe on the O2 mobile records for that morning, they asked him to think hard about what exactly had happened. Mobile phone technology has advanced so much in recent years that experts can prove indisputably which phone mast a mobile phone is nearest at the time of each communication made. The detectives illustrated that, at the same point in time that morning, Quearney's phone signal had bounced off a mast in the city centre, but Joe's had bounced off the mast within minutes of his home in Baldarragh. They asked him again – could he be wrong about his timing that morning, having seen a graph of the whereabouts of the two phones at the times the calls were made? The records showed that the times Quearney had given in his account of Joe's movements showed a disparity of thirty to forty minutes when compared to the phone records. Quearney conceded that it was possible that he was wrong, but he continued to insist that he did not remember it that way. When he was asked once again by the Gardaí what time he thought he had met Joe at the depot, he replied, 'I think it was nine-fifty a.m. or ten a.m.' When questioned under oath by the prosecution, he admitted in the witness box that the earliest he could definitely say that he had seen Joe O'Reilly at the depot on the morning of the murder was 11.00 a.m. Regardless, Quearney still insisted in the face of all the evidence that was put to him that that was simply how he remembered it.

Calmly, Vaughan Buckley then read from a statement Quearney had made to the Gardaí on 2 March 2006, in which he confirmed that he had been shown O2 reports concerning the locations of Joe's mobile phone on the day of the murder. 'From these reports I accept my original timing of seeing Joe O'Reilly at the Broadstone bus depot on 4 October could be wrong,' Quearney's statement read. 'I wish to add the only time that I can be definitely sure about seeing Mr O'Reilly was at the time I rang [a work colleague's] mobile phone. I accept the time of that phone call was ten fifty-nine a.m. on the fourth of October. That was at the very end of the inspection.'

When questioned, Quearney confirmed to the court that he had known about Joe's affair with Nikki Pelley. He was asked what Joe had told him to say if anybody questioned Joe's whereabouts while he was with his mistress. 'He told me if he was going out for the affair and if anyone rang to say he was "out of the office",' Quearney explained.

'Did you and Mr O'Reilly cover for each other at the office?' Vaughan Buckley asked.

'He'd cover if I headed off early and stuff like that,' Quearney answered.

The defence, Patrick Gageby, then asked him, 'Would you ever cover for anyone who murdered?'

'Absolutely not,' Quearney answered.

I was reminded of the irony of Joe's comments to journalist Jenny Friel when she asked him about Quearney. Joe stressed the fact that they were not friends; he claimed that the first thing he did when he got this job was fire one of his pals. He then claimed he got the job that Quearney probably felt was rightly his, so, Joe explained, Quearney certainly had no reason to cover for him. As Quearney said himself, it was quite usual for him to cover for Joe O'Reilly, and that made me very, very angry. The indescribable numbness I felt in the early weeks after Rachel's murder was taken over by anger as the real story came out of how Rachel was so horribly betrayed. I am still trying to come to terms with the level of anger I felt at times like these.

I was however very grateful that the truth was coming out in court before our eyes and the eyes of the world. They say that a picture paints a thousand words, and the truth of that saying was brought home to me as an engineer by the name of Enda Furlong demonstrated with a laptop linked to the flat-screen televisions in the court room how he could plot on a colour-coded map the movements of both Joe O'Reilly's and Derek Quearney's phones during the crucial times on the day of the murder.

Enda Furlong informed the court of the communications made and received on Joe O'Reilly's phone in chronological order between 08:12:57 and 15:24:57. The presentation showed coloured sections of the map lighting up as Joe's phone moved through different areas of mobile phone mast coverage. It very clearly traced Joe's journey from The Naul to work early on the morning of 4 October. It then showed his phone travelling west to Bluebell industrial estate, and then returning in a northerly direction back towards his home at the time of the murder. Eighteen minutes later, it showed him returning to the Broadstone depot in the north inner city and, later that day, he went back to his home in Baldarragh, The Naul, again. The map showed very clearly Joe's arrival and departure from The Naul area at 09.25 a.m. and 09.52 a.m., respectively. It was eerie to witness the area covered by the Murphy's Quarry mast lighting up. The colour blue was used to show the movements of Joe's phone, and Quearney's was marked in red, and the two phones were not near each other at the crucial time in question.

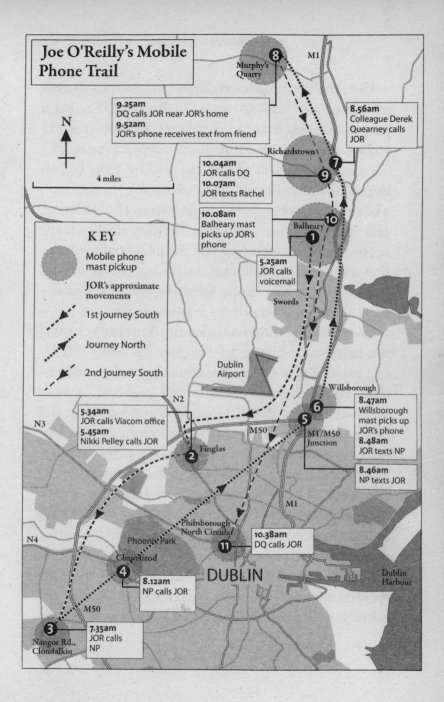

Joe O'Reilly's Mobile Phone Trail

M1

Murphy's Quarry

8

9.25am
DQ calls JOR near JOR's home
9.52am
JOR's phone receives text from friend

8.56am
Colleague Derek Quearney calls JOR

Richardstown

7
9

10.04am
JOR calls DQ
10.07am
JOR texts Rachel

10.08am
Balheary mast picks up JOR's phone

Balheary
10
1

5.25am
JOR calls voicemail

N

4 miles

KEY

Mobile phone mast pickup

JOR's approximate movements

- - - ► 1st journey South

······ ► Journey North

- - - ↙ 2nd journey South

Swords

Dublin Airport

Willsborough
6

8.47am
Willsborough mast picks up JOR's phone
8.48am
JOR texts NP

N2

5.34am
JOR calls Viacom office
5.45am
Nikki Pelley calls JOR

N3

Finglas
2

M50

M1/M50 Junction
5

8.46am
NP texts JOR

M1

N4

Phoenix Park

Phibsborough
North Circular

11

10.38am
DQ calls JOR

Chapelizod
4

8.12am
NP calls JOR

DUBLIN

Dublin Harbour

M50

Nangor Rd., Clondalkin
3

7.35am
JOR calls NP

The mobile phone records of Joe O'Reilly's phone on the day of the murder played a huge part in bringing him to justice, but the data that O2 collected did much more than expose Quearney's lies. Someone I will always be grateful to is Karim Benabdallah, a consultant working for the O2 network, who gave expert and indisputable evidence. His emphatic and confident delivery of his testimony meant a lot to us, as did the efforts of the team that worked alongside him, including Oliver Farrell from Vilicom, and Eddie Gleeson, to name a few – their hard work did not go unrewarded.

The mobile phone records put Joe at the scene of the crime at the time of the murder. Joe O'Reilly had no idea that day that technology had overtaken him. He thought he had it all planned out so thoroughly, but thank God he was so wrong. All of the emails and text messages from his mobile phone gave a perfect reconstruction of his whereabouts and text conversations in the months before and after Rachel's murder. The table on pages 225–9 shows the telephone records read aloud by the prosecution, detailing Joe O'Reilly's mobile phone use for 4 October 2004.

It made me feel sick to the pit of my stomach to see that not only had Joe been in contact with his mistress as he made his way out to kill his wife but,

Time of Call/ Text	Identity of Caller	Recipient	Type and duration of call	Nearest phone mast to Joe O'Reilly's phone	Location of phone being contacted
05.25:05	Joe O'Reilly	Voicemail	Call 2mins 9secs	Balheary	–
05.34:56	Joe O'Reilly	Viacom Office	Call 38secs	Finglas ESB	Bluebell Ind. Estate
05.45:14	Nikki Pelley	Joe O'Reilly	Call 27mins 43secs	Finglas Garda Stn.	Rathfarnham
07.35:16	Joe O'Reilly	Nikki Pelley (o)	Call 4mins 45secs	Nangor Road	–
08.12:57	Nikki Pelley	Joe O'Reilly	Call 25mins 57secs	Chapelizod	Rathfarnham
08.46:47	Nikki Pelley	Joe O'Reilly	Text	Airways, Junc. M1/M50	Milltown
08.48:14	Joe O'Reilly	Nikki Pelley	Text	Wills-borough	Milltown
08.56:51	Derek Quearney	Joe O'Reilly	Call 45secs	Richards-town	Chapelizod
08.58:59	Derek Quearney	Joe O'Reilly	Aborted call	Richards-town	No information
09.25:06	Derek Quearney	Joe O'Reilly	Call 2mins 6secs	Murphy's Quarry	Dominick Street
09.52:28	Kieran Gallagher	Joe O'Reilly	Text	Murphy's Quarry	Greystones
10.04:13	Joe O'Reilly	Derek Quearney	Call 8secs	Richards-town	North King Street

Time of Call/ Text	Identity of Caller	Recipient	Type and duration of call	Nearest phone mast to Joe O'Reilly's phone	Location of phone being contacted
10.07:30	Joe O'Reilly	Rachel O'Reilly	Text	Richardstown	Baldarragh
10.38:27	Derek Quearney	Joe O'Reilly	Call 54secs	North Circular Road	North King Street
11.02:05	Nikki Pelley	Joe O'Reilly	Voicemail 4secs	No information	Maiden out door office
11.05:17	Nikki Pelley	Joe O'Reilly	Call 3mins 29secs	Dominic Street	Maiden out door office
11.32:57	Cosmo Plastics	Joe O'Reilly	Call 16secs	Chapelizod	No information
12.01:23	Pfizer	Joe O'Reilly	Call 11secs	Killeen Road ESB	No information
12.06:01	Nikki Pelley	Joe O'Reilly	Call 27secs	Killeen Road ESB	Dundrum
12.59:59	Nikki Pelley	Joe O'Reilly	Text	Killeen Road ESB	No information
13.14:30	Creche	Joe O'Reilly	Call 3mins 8secs	Killeen Road ESB	The Naul
13.20:34	Joe O'Reilly	Rachel O'Reilly	Call 51secs	Killeen Road ESB	Baldarragh
13.21:41	Joe O'Reilly	Home phone	45secs	Inchicore	Baldarragh
13.22:36	Joe O'Reilly	Jackie O'Connor	Call 1min 12secs	Inchicore	No information

Time of Call/ Text	Identity of Caller	Recipient	Type and duration of call	Nearest phone mast to Joe O'Reilly's phone	Location of phone being contacted
13.24.29	Joe O'Reilly	Anthony Callaly	Call 1min 25secs	Inchicore	Collins Avenue
13.26:27	Joe O'Reilly	Rachel O'Reilly	Call 36secs	Chapelizod	Baldarragh
13.28:48	Joe O'Reilly	Tots United	Call 1min 57secs	Chapelizod	The Naul
13.40:14	Rose Callaly	Joe O'Reilly	Call 2mins 41secs	DG Motors, Navan Road	Collins Avenue
13.47:53	Joe O'Reilly	Rachel O'Reilly	Call 37secs	Poppintree	Baldarragh
13.48:31	Callaly home	Joe O'Reilly	Call 28secs	Airways M50	Collins Avenue
13.49:47	Joe O'Reilly	Anthony Callaly	Text	No information	–
13.53:18	Joe O'Reilly	Anthony Callaly	Call 23secs	Balheary	No information
13.57:06	Callaly home	Joe O'Reilly	Call 32secs	Richards-town	Collins Avenue
14.10:15	Joe O'Reilly	Anthony Callaly	Call 1min 34secs	Richards-town	No information
14.13:33	Anthony Callaly	Joe O'Reilly	Call 18secs	Murphy's Quarry	No information
14.20:17	Anthony Callaly	Joe O'Reilly	Voicemail 32secs	Murphy's Quarry	No information
14.23:00	O'Reilly home	Joe O'Reilly	Call 3secs	Murphy's Quarry	Collins Avenue

Time of Call/ Text	Identity of Caller	Recipient	Type and duration of call	Nearest phone mast to Joe O'Reilly's phone	Location of phone being contacted
14.43:24	Joe O'Reilly	Anne O'Reilly	Call 48secs	Murphy's Quarry	No information
15.21:40	Nikki Pelley	Joe O'Reilly	Call 1min 14secs	Murphy's Quarry	Maiden Outdoor Office
15.24:36	Derek Quearney	Joe O'Reilly	Call 14secs	Murphy's Quarry	Killeen Road
15.24:54	Voicemail	Joe O'Reilly	Voicemail	Murphy's Quarry	No information
15.53:32	Viacom	Joe O'Reilly	Call 32secs	Stamullen, Co. Meath	Ind. Estate
15.55:32	Derek Quearney	Joe O'Reilly	Call 1min 12secs	Four Knocks	No information
16.07:07	Cosmo Plastics	Joe O'Reilly	No information	Dunleer	No information
16.08:28	Cosmo Plastics	Joe O'Reilly	Call 18secs	Dunleer	No information
16.33:38	Joe O'Reilly	Nikki Pelley	Call 5mins 48secs	Dunleer	Landline
16.54:24	Det Supt Michael Hoare	Joe O'Reilly	Call 1min 58secs	Dunleeer	Murphy's Quarry
17.22:29	Joe O'Reilly	Nikki Pelley	Call 4mins 39secs	Dunleer	No information
17.41:54	Joe O'Reilly	Nikki Pelley	Text	Dunleer	No information

Time of Call/ Text	Identity of Caller	Recipient	Type and duration of call	Nearest phone mast to Joe O'Reilly's phone	Location of phone being contacted
17.51:45	Nikki Pelley	Joe O'Reilly	Text	Dunleer	No information
17.52:02	Joe O'Reilly	Nikki Pelley	Text	Dunleer	No information
18.28:44	Nikki Pelley	Joe O'Reilly	Text	Dunleer	No information
18.51:02	Joe O'Reilly	Nikki Pelley	Failed text message	–	No information
18.56:14	Nikki Pelley	Joe O'Reilly	Text	Dunleer	No information

Derek Quearney: work colleague and friend of Joe O'Reilly

Anthony Callaly: Rachel's brother

Jackie O'Connor: Rachel's best friend

Rose Callaly: Rachel's mother

Viacom: Joe O'Reilly's employers

Creche: The crèche that Rachel's youngest attended

once he had cleaned himself up and left the mother of his two children for dead – maybe she was still alive, we will never know – he drove away and, just a few minutes later, sent her a text asking if she and the children had had a good night's sleep. He knew full well what he had done, and that Rachel would never hear from anybody ever again.

Joe O'Reilly thought that he had covered his tracks when it came to his mobile phone. He had used an old handset that morning and made sure to switch the SIM card from his normal phone and put it in the old handset. The police found that old handset in his mother's house in Dunleer. What Joe did not know was that the handset he had left in his mother's house actually had an identification number on it, so each time his phone registered a text or a call from the nearest mast, the number of the handset registered as well as the SIM card number. Detective Garda John Clancy confirmed that the experts could say without doubt that this was the phone used at the relevant time in question on the day of his wife's murder.

Another demonstration as to how sick and evil Joe is would come later, in the form of a voicemail he left on Rachel's phone on 4 November, exactly a month after he killed her. He called at 08.25 a.m. that morning, and said:

Hi, Rach, it's me, Joe. I am very very sorry for the early-morning phone call. This time a month ago you were probably doing what I am doing now, getting the kids ready for school. Now you are so cold. The sun was out. It was a normal day, you had less than two hours to live. I just want to go back in time and say I love you. I don't want to live without you, and that's the truth. I miss you and I love you. Sleep well and rest in peace. I have to get the kids ready now, I love you and miss you. Chat later, bye.

Rachel's phone, of course, was with the Gardaí when this message was left – they had kept it since the murder. Joe probably thought that he was fooling them while he carried on his 'new life' with his mistress.

It was a relief to find that all witnesses for the prosecution had been called. Soon, the defence called their witnesses, including Joseph O'Shea. He had attended Greendale Community School in Kilbarrack, the same school as Derek and Joe O'Reilly. O'Shea said that it was only during the trial that he read in the papers that Joe was claiming to have been at the Broadstone bus depot at the time of the murder. Joseph O'Shea said it was like a light bulb went off in his head, and he suddenly remembered seeing Joe outside the Broadstone depot at some stage. He discussed his memory with his family and his colleagues and decided to go to the Gardaí. In his statement dated July 2007, Joseph O'Shea said that he could not be clear as to when he had actually seen Joe O'Reilly. He said that he could not remember the date that he saw him, or what time it had been. All he could say for certain was that it was lashing rain on the morning he drove past the depot, and he had seen Joe O'Reilly there. Everything started to come together. The jury was then reminded of the evidence given by meteorological expert John Doyle as to the weather conditions in Dublin on Monday 4 October 2004. We all thought back, and realized the significance of that seemingly irrelevant evidence given in the early stages of the trial: it had been clear and sunny in Dublin that morning. Judge Barry White then asked Joseph O'Shea if he could remember what clothes Joe was wearing on the morning he said he saw him but O'Shea could not. When the judge asked him if he could remember if Joe was wearing any rain gear, O'Shea replied, 'I just know I seen him.'

As they finished with the witnesses and we waited to find out what would come next, Rachel's whole life was going through my mind as we sat in that courtroom. My mind would take me back years: I would remember Rachel's face and her happy, shining eyes, and I could almost feel myself back in those warm summer days when we used to go camping with our friends and their children. As I sat there in that stuffy, crowded courtroom, I would picture Rachel along with the rest of the children, creating make-believe dens and playing happily. We were so careful to keep them at a safe distance and away from danger, while still letting them have enough freedom not to feel stifled. We would watch them all play so innocently and we were completely content. I could picture her beautiful brown little face as she would hold up her plate for her share of the sausages, pudding and burgers we would cook on the bonfire we used to light when it got dark at the campsite. I remembered fishing out the potatoes wrapped in foil that we had thrown into the embers to cook. The children went to sleep in the tents beside the campfire an hour or so before us adults let the fire burn out before we turned in. Even the task of collecting brush and firewood each day was a source of fun for them. Rachel loved these camping trips so much, and it was something she was looking forward to sharing with the children. Shortly before she died, she bought Jim a new tent for his birthday and she was hoping to bring the children camping with their grandad, but sadly they did not get to experience this. Sitting on that bench in Court Number 2, I could picture the bright blaze of the beautiful yellow gorse bush and smell the coconut scent that filled the air. It brought me back to happier times, and it seemed so unbelievable that her happy life could have come to this horrific end.

It was Rachel's presence in all of these family times that was uppermost in my mind during the trial, the carefree days she loved so much. It helped me in some way to remember that she did have happiness in her life, and I remember I would think to myself, if only I could have the chance to do it all over again. It would remind me that we really only have a loan of them for those few childhood years, but that when they set out in life, you never think that your children will be denied the joy you experienced in rearing them.

18. Guilty

After four long weeks of going to the court each morning, we knew that the long-awaited verdict would soon be made known. I was so stressed on that last day, I really could not say how Joe O'Reilly was handling it. I was still greatly disturbed by everything we had learned during the trial, and now more than ever I prayed hard for justice for Rachel. Representing the prosecution, Dominick McGinn spent two hours outlining the enormous amount of evidence that had been put before the jury. He acknowledged that the evidence that had been gathered against Joe O'Reilly was circumstantial and explained that, when it was all put together, it proved Joe O'Reilly's guilt beyond a reasonable doubt.

He described the different pieces of evidence as being like separate strands of a rope: the individual strands might not be strong enough on their own, but when you tie them all together they are, he said. As he reminded the jury of the evidence showing Rachel's Renault Scenic returning to the house after she had dropped the children to the school and crèche, he pointed out to the jury it was evident Rachel had been attacked as soon as she entered her home, as she still had her car keys clutched in her hand when her body was found. He reminded them of the violent nature of Rachel's death as described by Dr Marie Cassidy and Dr Diane Daly, and how the Gardaí had ruled out the burglary theory. Dominick McGinn went on to explain that the absence of blood or DNA either inside or outside the house showed that whoever killed Rachel had not panicked, but took their time to take a shower, cleaning off the blood before making a getaway. He also pointed out the significance of the large amount of cash left behind: €860 found in a box in the utility room and €400 in Rachel's handbag, a sum of money that no burglar would have left behind. He also explained that the few items taken from the house and found in a ditch near by had no blood on them and looked as if they had been planted there. He pointed out that the people Joe had mentioned who might have held a grudge against either himself or Rachel had solid alibis for the day of the murder. He told the jury that the blood found on the washing-machine door had turned out to belong to Rachel's half-brother Thomas.

Dominick McGinn also addressed the issue of Joe's affair with Nikki Pelley. This was not just an affair for sex as they were trying to make it out to be, and there was ample evidence that they were planning to have a future together. I froze in my seat as he reminded the jury of the two separate halves of Visa cards that were previously shown in evidence during the trial. He spoke of the affectionate tone of the text messages Joe had sent which left no doubt as to how he felt about Nikki Pelley. Then there were the emails between Joe and his sister, Anne O'Reilly Jnr, which showed quite clearly how he felt about Rachel and what was really going on. Mr McGinn said that those emails revealed what Joe really thought – 'That's what his real state of mind was, and that is motive, ladies and gentlemen,' Mr McGinn explained to the jury.

He went on to say that Joe's alibi was a lie, as the mobile phone evidence proved that Joe was at his home out in Baldarragh at the time of Rachel's murder. This had been proven by the discovery of the SIM card and handset that had been used at the time of the murder, so Joe could not claim that his phone was cloned. Joe had admitted to the Gardaí from the start that he had his mobile phone with him at all times, and Mr McGinn highlighted the calls and texts to and from Joe's mobile phone on the day of the murder, explaining once again how the experts had proven that it would have been impossible for a call received by Joe in the Broadstone depot to have been routed through the mast at Murphy's Quarry. He then discussed Quearney's claim that he had met Joe in the depot between 09.50 a.m. and 10.00 a.m., but then admitted that he might be mistaken about the time. The only time he could be certain that he actually saw Joe at the Broadstone depot was at 10.59 a.m., when Joe stood beside him as he called a work colleague on his mobile phone.

Dominick McGinn put it to the jury that Joe's alibi was provided by an unreliable witness. He instructed the jury to remember Derek Quearney had worked with Joe O'Reilly for a number of years and had covered for O'Reilly's affair, lying to cover up for Joe when he went out to meet Nikki Pelley. He reminded the jury about all of the CCTV footage that showed that Joe was not where he said he was that morning and how he lied about his alibi.

Mr McGinn stressed that the only person with a reason to kill Rachel was Joe, describing him as 'the only person with a motive'. 'The only rational explanation is that Mr O'Reilly killed his wife. Because of that, I suggest you cannot have a reasonable doubt. If you have no reasonable doubt, then you must convict him.'

I felt sick as Patrick Gageby rose to his feet, and I wished my hearing would go so I did not have to listen to him. He reminded the jury of the extreme nature of what they were being asked to do. He told them that the decision they made in this case would be 'irreversible', and he warned them that the conclusion they came to would stand for all time. The finality of his words was imprinted on my brain, but I now wonder how he could be allowed to make such a statement to the jury at such a crucial time. We soon found out that it is the constitutional right of every citizen who is found guilty of a crime and is sentenced to appeal that decision. Depending on whether their appeal is successful or not, the original jury decision can be reversed.

Mr Gageby acknowledged that many people might not like Joe O'Reilly because he had an affair and, as he put it, said 'nasty things' about his wife: 'So he lets off steam, so he uses bad language, which is really unpleasant – so what? Where is the homicide?' Mr Gageby asked the jury. He told them how the prosecution had set out to discredit Joe O'Reilly at every opportunity because he had an affair with Nikki Pelley. He continued, saying that the prosecution's case consisted of 'a lot of innuendo and allegations, but only a little bit of substance'. He addressed the jury, stating that, if Joe O'Reilly was not having an affair or being disloyal to Rachel, it would be a lot easier to give him the benefit of the doubt. Gageby made a wide gesture with his hands and said to the jury, 'If he was incredibly likeable, did a lot of work for charity or had won medals for Ireland, you would approach this case differently, but this is not a court of morality, it is a court of law. You are now the judges. You are in the driving seat.' I could not believe what I was hearing. I had no doubt that there was anybody there who was judging Joe O'Reilly on his morals, but if he was the kind of person that Mr Gageby was describing, I doubt that he would ever be standing in the dock accused of his wife's murder. Knowing all I knew about Joe O'Reilly, things that the jury would never hear, made it all the harder to hear.

As Mr Gageby then referred to the amount of media coverage the case had attracted, he urged the jury not to reach the verdict he said the press wanted just because it would sell more newspapers. In the past forty or fifty years, he did not think he knew of a case that had been covered by so many journalists or seen so many people queue up to get into the court, he said. He said that he always approaches a case with the view that publicity is unwelcome, because the journalists try to skew things. 'You must reach a decision in this case without any consideration to the publicity,' he said. Gageby continued that the most difficult thing to do is something which is unpopular, advising the jury to examine their consciences and reach the right decision. During his speech against the press's involvement, I kept thinking how Joe O'Reilly had courted the media, secure in the assumption that he had gotten away with it. Now that the truth had started to emerge, of course, the media had no intention of backing off after that, as Joe had involved himself from the very start.

Mr Gageby indicated to the jury that, if the prosecution was right in its calculations, Joe O'Reilly would have had only eighteen minutes to kill Rachel, take a shower to wash away the blood, get dressed and get into his car. 'From nine forty-one a.m. to nine fifty-nine a.m.,' he said, 'everything had to be done in that time if the prosecution is right.' Gageby once again told the jury that the prosecution's case was based on a large amount of suspicion with a little bit of science. I disagreed; the scientific evidence was very strong, and the prosecution had an awful lot more than scientific evidence to uphold their case. As Mr Gageby went on to dismiss most of the prosecution's case, the reality of the terrible events hit me again. It was very difficult to have to sit and listen as the defence trivialized and made light of some of the evidence put forward by the prosecution. It almost seemed at times as if the terrible death that Rachel had been subjected to and the awful way in which she had been treated and spoken about was being made to look as if it was normal, that somehow, Joe's behaviour before her death could be excused. I would have to reassure myself deep down that this is the way the game is played, there has to be a defence or there could not be a trial, but I wish there was a better way than trying to make all the cruel behaviour she was subjected to appear as normal. The defence, after all their intensive searching and investigation, could only produce two witnesses, Derek Quearney and Joseph O'Shea, neither of whom had any evidence whatsoever to prove Joe O'Reilly's innocence. Mr Gageby did his very best, and if it had been possible to actually discredit any part of the huge amount of evidence put forward by the prosecution, there was no better man to do it than Mr Gageby – but thankfully he could not produce what did not exist.

As I sat there on that bench, I could see the faces of all the various witnesses and their damning evidence pass before my eyes, and I remember thinking, *Whatever happens now, I will always be grateful to every one of those witnesses who had the courage to stand up and tell the truth in Rachel's defence.* I went home that evening in a state of numbness, bracing myself for a tense and difficult time for us.

The following morning we went in not knowing how many more such mornings we would have to endure. I remember thinking that if Joe O'Reilly had told the truth, none of this would be taking place and everybody would have been spared all this agony, but I may as well have wished for the moon. As we were sitting on that now-familiar bench, Justice Barry White made his entrance. He is not a big man, and yet, as he sat down and started to give his summation in his strong, clear voice, he could have been seven foot, he commanded such respect. He told the jury of nine men and two women that his instruction was final. He said with a wistful sort of a smile that he was like the Pope in matters of faith, infallible as far they were concerned, here in matters of law. He told them that Joe O'Reilly was entitled to the presumption of innocence, that he did not have to prove that he had not murdered his wife Rachel, but that it was up to the State to prove him guilty beyond a reasonable doubt.

Justice White asked them to imagine what it would feel like to be in Joe O'Reilly's shoes and how they would feel if they were found guilty on the evidence that was put before them. If they felt that they would not have got justice on that evidence, then the State had failed to prove his guilt beyond a reasonable doubt. The judge pointed out parts of the prosecution's case that in his opinion the jury should disregard, as there could be simple explanations for them, and it was his opinion that such evidence did not point to either guilt or innocence. At times like these, I felt the balance was so in Joe's favour that I found it hard to sit still.

He continued and told the jury not to assume anything about Joe O'Reilly just because he did not take the stand to defend himself, that they were to make their decision on the evidence that they heard in the court and nothing else. There was no obligation on the defendant to either give evidence or answer any questions that were put to him by the

Gardaí, so 'you should give no weight to the fact that Joe O'Reilly did not go into the witness box in this case,' he said. Justice White informed the jury that in this case, the defendant did actually answer questions from the Gardaí, and that they would have notes of those.

Just after 3 p.m. that Friday 20 July, the jury was sent out to deliberate a verdict. Justice White told them that, if they did not reach a verdict by 7 p.m., they would be sent to a hotel for the night. The jury arose and walked out of the box across to the big door to the right, and, while we had become accustomed to their coming and going through that very door over the last few weeks, this time was different. It is a difference that is hard to put into words, and again I found it hard to breathe. I wanted to be anywhere but in that court. We knew that this was it. The jury had heard all of the evidence and would now have no contact with anyone except the Gardaí, who would look after them until their decision had been reached. I kept thinking that we should not be sitting here in this stuffy, airless courtroom in the middle of summer in these awful circumstances. Rachel, our beloved daughter, should be at home in her back garden having a barbecue with the husband she had loved so much and her two beloved children. All of their lives should have stretched out happily before them. All the ingredients were there for them all to be happy, they were so lucky, I thought. Dear God, what went wrong and why? The thought uppermost in my mind was 'Please God, let Rachel have justice.' I cannot tell you how important that was to us. I only know it had become essential and it became our reason to go on. I have often said there were no winners when it came to Rachel's loss. No person in their right mind would choose to be involved in a case like this, I thought. All we could do now was wait. We were so tense that each time there were knocks on the door from the jury, my heart would jump, but each time it was a false alarm: the foreman needed copies of charts, or the jury was seeking permission for a cigarette break.

I am sure that the atmosphere must have been very stressful for the jury, as theirs was an unenviable task. At 7 p.m. that evening, they had not reached a verdict, and, as Justice White had promised, they were sent to a hotel for a night. Joe O'Reilly left the courts for what was to be his last night of freedom. None of our family got much sleep that night, we were so restless and stressed about the possibilities for the future and the many unanswered questions about the past. In the beginning of the trial, when I could not close my eyes or sleep at night, I used to wish Joe O'Reilly would be confronted each night of his life before he closed his eyes with what he had done to the blameless loving mother of his two children. I would wish for him that the horrific scene that still haunts me would be the last thing to come before his eyes and the reality of what he had done will never leave him. That is still my wish.

We arose early the next morning, a Saturday. Charlie, my brother, called again and brought us to the court. Spectators were crowding the Four Courts, trying to get a place in Court Number 2 to witness the proceedings. It was jammed, and what little air there was in the court room seemed to disappear between all the people. Between the heat and the lack of air, the time crawled. I remember feeling every second of every minute of that day tick by as we waited for the jury to return.

By lunchtime, when proceedings were formally stopped, it was with relief that we went over to O'Shea's pub, The Merchant, to have our lunch. We had gone there every day of the trial, and it was a welcome break for us. It's a lovely old pub right on the corner as you cross the bridge over the River Liffey. From day one, they kept a large table in a quiet corner for us, and we just had to ring ahead to let them know each day how many of us were coming. It was a great help to us, and they looked after us very well.

When we got back to the courts, our family sat outside Court Number 2, where we found some space in an alcove under the stairs near the reception. It was just off the Round Room, but it was a spot that allowed us a little bit of privacy while we waited for the jury to return. I remember a man who worked in the courts approaching us at one stage; I think he felt sorry for us. He suggested we should go off somewhere and have a cup of coffee or something. We said that we were afraid to go any further in case the jury returned, but he offered to ring us on our mobile phone if they did. We decided that we would stay and wait there while some of friends went out and brought coffee and refreshments back to us, as everything within the courts was closed for the weekend. It was a very surreal feeling, waiting there for the jury to come back in with their verdict. I remember having great confidence that the jury would return with the right verdict, but being equally sure that, whatever it took, I would continue to fight for justice for Rachel even if it took over my life.

Once it passed six o'clock, I started to get very

anxious. I was willing them with all my might to come back and return to their seats, and, at 6.40 p.m., a court official ran out and beckoned us to go in. I felt shaky as we took our places. The registrar went into the jury room and returned after just a few minutes, nodding to the legal teams to indicate that there was a verdict. We sat there as if frozen. Justice White entered and took his place. The foreman handed the registrar a folded piece of paper, and as the registrar read out the verdict that found Joe O'Reilly guilty of killing his wife, the whole courtroom erupted. The feeling of relief that at last it had ended is indescribable. I turned and hugged and kissed Jim, as at last our family heard that one word from the court registrar as she read out the verdict we had been awaiting for so long: GUILTY. We all broke down and were hugging and kissing one another. I remember hugging some of the men who had worked so hard and given so much of themselves to get justice for Rachel. I do not know how Joe O'Reilly reacted to the verdict, I did not look at him. I only know I was glad that justice was done but I felt a deep regret that the nightmare had happened at all, it had all been so unnecessary – and for what?

The uproar was so much that eventually the judge ordered the court to calm down. Justice Barry White ordered Joe O'Reilly to stand. 'You have been found guilty by the jury. The sentence prescribed for murder is one of imprisonment for life. I am now imposing that sentence on you.' Judge Barry White thanked the jury and spoke of the pressure they had to deal with during the trial. He also excused them from jury duty for the rest of their lives, adding that, in all his years as a barrister and a judge, he had never seen a trial attract such intense media coverage. Before dismissing the court for the last time, he gave me permission to read my victim impact statement. I read the statement on behalf of my family that each one of us had contributed to. It was very important for me to have been given the opportunity to read this statement. It was a relief to have sat in that same seat where all of the evidence had been delivered and to be able to express some of the trauma that we felt, some of what we as a family had lost, and what we had endured over the weeks of the trial learning what our Rachel had gone through. I sat in the witness box once again and read:

Almost three years ago, Rachel kissed her beloved children goodbye, and for the next twenty minutes was subjected to the most horrific, violent and barbaric attack – that no human being should ever have to go through. We are haunted by the thoughts of what happened to our beautiful daughter and sister that morning. From that moment on, the lives of everyone who knew Rachel and loved her were thrown into turmoil.

Even though justice has been done, our grief and distress will never diminish. Rachel was a truly beautiful, loving, caring and capable girl who has left so many memories, and she meant so much to so many – her aunts, uncles, cousins, niece and nephews and many friends. Each one of us has been traumatized by feelings of helplessness, shock, grief, and the horrific reality is that we can do nothing to bring her back. That is the hardest part of our pain.

Not only did Rachel leave without saying goodbye, she also left her beloved children confused, scared and angry. We feel heartbroken, as the biggest damage will surely be left at their door as they live their lives without the guidance and counselling of their best friend. Rachel was never away from their side, and her harrowing loss has left a huge void in both their lives and our lives.

Every day we find it so very difficult to accept the devastation of her death. We struggle to come to terms with the fact that she is now gone for ever. There are days when we feel overwhelmed by grief. Sleepless nights, nightmares and panic attacks have become the norm for us – we often waken traumatized with fear by the images of terror, violence and brutality – and we wonder if we will ever return to some sense of a normal life.

We lost Rachel at the young age of thirty years, and we are devastated knowing we will never be able to share with her the enjoyment of all the milestones she was so looking forward to in her life, and the possibility of one day sharing with her the enjoyment of seeing her own grandchildren. As a parent it is devastating to lose a child, but under these circumstances, at times it is unbearable.

Rachel, if I could have given my life for you that awful day, I would have. You are such a big part of our life. Thank you for the short lifetime which should have been so much longer and full of so many more happy memories. We treasure the memories of shared times with you. We miss and love you so much and not a day passes without you being remembered so lovingly.

We hope you can now rest in peace, my darling, your loving Mam and Dad, brothers, sister and sisters-in-law, Declan and Denise, Paul and Denise, Ann and Anthony and your two little children.

The scene of all the well-wishers and family who thronged the courts to offer their support to us was astonishing – it seemed to take for ever for us to make our way through the happy crowd to leave the courtroom for the final time.

I will never forget the moment that we walked out of the court that summer evening. It was over, and we were walking out into the fresh air and into freedom. In the Round Room, we were met by our extended family, including my sister Susan, brother Tony and sister Sindy, who had come in from California for the end of the trial, and Rachel's friends, and then by dozens of photographers who were waiting for us to leave the court. Some of Rachel's supporters who we didn't know told us that they had raced down to the court when they heard the verdict. Nothing will make us forget the support we received throughout the whole ordeal, and, after more than four weeks in court, for now, it was over.

19. The Appeal

It was exactly one year to the day after a jury found Joe O'Reilly guilty of murdering Rachel that a date was given for his appeal hearing. The date was set for 18 December 2008, and we tried desperately not to think about it.

On the morning of Thursday 18 December, as we prepared ourselves to face yet another day in the courts, I felt it was as if we were being punished yet again. It felt like we'd gone back in time to one of the hardest periods of our lives. Once again, Charlie drove us to the Four Courts. It was very comforting to have him with us and that we did not have the additional stress of having to book a taxi after one didn't turn up on the first day of the trial. More importantly, it was a huge comfort to know that my brother was there for us the whole time.

When we arrived at the Four Courts, there was a huge crowd of photographers standing in horrendous weather, trying to take pictures in gale-force winds and lashing rain. The weather reflected the way I was feeling as we hurried as quickly as we could to escape being drenched right through. The same awful feeling had once again taken over. When we entered the corridors of the Four Courts, it was mayhem. The door to Court Number 6 was locked, so the corridor outside was jammed with people, some who had arrived at 7 a.m., hoping to be able to witness the proceedings.

At about ten minutes to eleven the doors opened, and everyone took their place in the small and by now very crowded courtroom. I was conscious of the large media presence as we entered, and it seemed we had only just sat down when Joe O'Reilly was led in flanked by prison guards and handcuffed to one of them. When I saw him arriving chained to an officer, I felt a pang of pity for him, but what he had done flashed through my head so fast, my life split into two – the before and after of what he did to my child – and my pity did not last long. I tried not to look as Joe and his sister laughed and joked as we sat waiting for the three judges to arrive. Eventually they did, and the proceedings started.

The Court of Criminal Appeal was led by Chief Justice John Murray, Justice Roderick Murphy and Justice Patrick McCarthy, who all sat listening intently as counsel for Joe O'Reilly, Patrick Gageby, outlined his grounds of appeal. The team had originally submitted eleven aspects of his trial which they claimed were flawed, but Patrick Gageby had withdrawn a number of them, including a dispute over whether Joe and his sister Anne had actually written the poisonous emails, in which he suggested that the emails should not have been put before the jury as they had been sent in June 2004, four months before the murder.

As they went through grounds for Joe's appeal, I felt Rachel's presence in the room. It was torturous to have to listen to their outrageous reasoning. I realized how cruel the law really is, and how it feels like it has nothing to do with justice. No one mentioned one word about justice for Rachel and her two children. It was outrageous to think that Joe O'Reilly's legal team were explaining that his trial was somehow unfair. Joe was given the opportunity to get up in the witness box to plead his case and defend himself but he did not choose to do so. Joe was afforded a very fair trial presided over by a judge who gave him the benefit of the doubt throughout the trial, and at times it seemed like things were far too much in his favour. He had one of the best defence barristers in the land and a jury that took their time in order to come to a very fair and unanimous decision. I will be for ever grateful to that jury for being so conscientious and giving such a fair verdict, but Joe's legal team had put together a list of objections to chip away at the jury's decision.

Joe's defence said that only evidence that referred to his state of mind at the time of the murder should have been permitted. His legal team was trying to make out that his state of mind in relation to Rachel had somehow miraculously changed in the four months since the hate-filled emails between him and his sister. Between the emails and Joe's November deadline from his mistress, it was evident to me that the only change to his state of mind had taken him from bad to worse. Needless to say, his counsel objected to the use of much of the evidence about Nikki Pelley, including that the jury should not have heard that Joe had spent the night with her after *The Late Late Show*, in which he appealed to the public for help in catching Rachel's killer.

In relation to other cases, I know that, whenever possible, the jury and the public at large are prevented from knowing about any previous convictions that the accused may have, even if the accused committed a string of similar horrific acts before they are eventually brought to trial. This is done so that no innocent person is convicted because of past crimes, and so that the jury bases their findings on the evidence heard in court and nothing else. Knowing some of the evidence that was not allowed to go before the jury, however, I am still very confused as to why so much is hidden. It was another moment in the trial in which it was clear to me that the law stands on the side of the accused, and in this case on the side of a murderer.

Thankfully, counsel for the prosecution, Denis Vaughan Buckley, could then remind everyone at the hearing that the awful emails were raised in the original trial to show how Joe and Anne O'Reilly Jnr felt about Rachel. Furthermore, other evidence proved that Nikki Pelley's role in the case was very important to understanding Joe's motivation to kill Rachel. Before he murdered her, he had ceased to consider her as the mother of their two children and would regularly refer to them in communications with Nikki Pelley as his children with her – a ready-made family for their new life together, as if

Rachel had never existed. How anybody could consider such inhuman behaviour as normal is just beyond me. There should be no hiding place or support for anybody capable of such behaviour, and Joe O'Reilly's well-documented manipulation of his wife long before he murdered her ensured that his dreams of sailing off to start a new life have turned to dust.

I suppose what makes me feel so helpless is the fact that I know what Joe O'Reilly is capable of and what he did to Rachel, and yet, after his attempt at courting the media turned against him, he started to demand his rights – particularly his right to privacy. This from a man who took his wife's right to life when he killed her, and whose subsequent trial destroyed her right to privacy. During his trial, he did not reveal one scrap of pity as Rachel's life with him was exposed for the whole world to see. The most private parts of Rachel's life and the many ways she was betrayed were read out and exposed for a packed courtroom, and Joe couldn't even show a flicker of contrition for what he had done, and what he was doing to her now. But *he* could have ended it all by admitting in the beginning what he had done, thus giving her memory the dignity she so deserved.

Joe O'Reilly's cruel arrogance will never let this

happen. He will deny everything until the bitter end. I do not know what makes his kind tick, or how he perceives the world, but the pain that he inflicts on others doesn't even seem to register with him. He has never at any time shown any remorse or admitted to any wrong-doing in relation to Rachel, and I sincerely hope that, unless he does that, he will spend the rest of his days in prison. He gave up his right to freedom the day he carried out his heinous act of brutality and deserves no mercy as long as he continues to deny his actions. At least he has life, even if it is not the one he would have chosen. It is certainly the life he deserves. But for his own ruthless action, Rachel would be alive, their children would have been saved so much trauma in their young lives, and would still have their mother with them, and Joe would be a free man and could have moved on with his own life. I wonder if he ever reflects on this.

I used to think that after the trial we would feel some sense of closure and perhaps move on to a more normal life once again. The painful truth is that we now know that will never happen. We will pick up the threads of our lives with the help of our family and friends, but it can never be as it once was, and the pain simply never goes away. It is something that only those involved in similar situations can identify with. It cannot ever be over.

When the hearing was finished we had another agonizing wait, never knowing when the date for the judgement on the appeal would be revealed. It was exactly one week before Christmas 2008, and we were trying our best to look ahead to the holiday season now that we had the ordeal of the appeal hearing behind us. It was without a doubt the most stressful and disorganized Christmas I have ever experienced.

It seemed like an eternity passed as we tried to get through each day and live as normally as we could. As New Year's Eve was approaching yet again, Jim was looking forward to our annual gathering of friends on 31 December. I tried to remain positive, but part of me wanted the new year to hurry up and come so that the legal ordeals would be behind us. Deep down, at times I wished I could just opt out of life completely, as it all seemed so futile and painful. I have discovered during all of this that life has to be lived, even if your heart is breaking, and somehow the will to go on grows slowly inside of you. You learn to recognize that safe feeling of being needed by the people who love you, and you learn to live once again. It was as if all the prayers that people had been offering up for us carried us over the worst parts until we got the strength back to carry on.

The festivities passed, and now another new year stretched before us. Since Rachel's death, I always feel a reluctance to look to the future because I am reminded constantly of how unpredictable life can be and worry at what could await us. I hope that feeling will fade in time, and that we can once again look to the coming months and years with confidence, but for now we just had to wait for the decision on the appeal.

Thank God we received the court date for the appeal decision just two days before it was scheduled to be heard. It was a great relief to all of us. It was just as well it was only two days' notice, as knowing it was coming was very stressful on us, and none of us got much sleep during that time. In those two days, we were left feeling drained and we tried to distract ourselves by keeping busy, but still the time seemed to stand still and we were wishing it was all over. We received calls from around the country, some from people who we had never met, all wishing us good luck and sending their messages of encouragement. I asked people to keep up the prayers, as I felt it was a great help.

As we prepared once again to go through all the agony we had endured too many times before, Charlie arrived in his taxi to take us to the Four Courts on the morning of 6 March 2009, the day the judgement on Joe's appeal would be given. Time does not make this any easier – in fact, it just compounds the feelings of grief we all carry since Rachel's loss.

I felt numb as we made that now so familiar journey for what I was hoping would be the last time. Rachel was very much in evidence that morning, and we could feel her presence amongst us. I prayed that justice would not fail and hoped to God that good would once again overcome evil.

We entered the now very packed courtroom and took our places. We had not been sitting there for long before Joe O'Reilly was led into court in handcuffs as he attempted once more to cheat justice. I remember feeling that I could not bear to look at him. His arrogance in even considering that he had been wronged or was entitled to any more than the very fair and even-handed treatment he had received just made me feel ill as we waited in that stomach-churning void and tried to pray for the right outcome.

Jim sat by my side, trying to remain calm. The

boys, Declan, Paul and Anthony, wrestled with their own thoughts and emotions but thankfully they had their partners by their sides for support. I was very aware of Ann as she sat beside me and I could feel her pain. I prayed to God that this would be the end of it, and that life would hold better and happier days for her. We sat through the ordeal of waiting as the press and interested members of the public and people from the courts continued to fill the packed courtroom even more. It all had a surreal feeling about it, a feeling of total unreality.

Much to our relief, the three appeal judges made their entrance, and the proceedings began. When the Chief Justice, John Murray, started to read the judgement, I held my breath. Thankfully we did not have to endure a long court session, because suddenly, after a brief summing-up of the appeal grounds, I was relieved to hear Chief Justice Murray dismiss the application on all grounds, and a thirty-four-page judgement was circulated to all present in the court room.

In their judgement, the three judges outlined their reasons for dismissing each aspect of Joe O'Reilly's appeal. They decided that there was no reason why a jury should not know that a suspect had exercised the right to remain silent while being interviewed, as Joe O'Reilly had done. They made a point of the fact that juries often see the accused choosing not to answer questions by not taking the stand, and this was the same. The judges also agreed that the prosecutor, Denis Vaughan Buckley, had acted properly by not suggesting that the jury should draw any conclusions from Joe O'Reilly's decision to remain silent when being questioned.

They also discounted Joe's claim that the Gardaí should have cautioned him before he gave his statement, the statement in which he lied about his movements on the day he murdered Rachel. Joe O'Reilly's team argued that he had clearly been a suspect when he made his statement two days after the murder on 6 October 2004, and, as a result, the Gardaí should have read him his rights. But the appeal judges decided that it was not clear whether Joe O'Reilly was a suspect so early in the investigation. Joe's team also tried to discredit vital mobile phone evidence that proved that Joe had made the journey from his place of work in town to his home, which the judges rejected. The judges also rejected claims that no evidence had been given to prove that his mobile phone service provider, O2, was licensed in Ireland. The original testimony from O2's representative had made clear to the jury that the company did indeed have a licence, and the evidence was allowed to stand. The defence claimed that CCTV analysis from expert witness Andrew Laws was flawed because no comparison had been made to show that cars on the footage could be any model other than Joe's Fiat Marea. But the judges ruled that the claim was irrelevant, because Andrew Laws had only said that it was 'possible' that the car in the CCTV imagery belonged to Joe O'Reilly.

The last part of the appeal was that the jury should not have seen the poisonous emails between Joe and his sister Anne. The three judges dismissed this, too, saying that the contents of the emails showed that his contempt for Rachel had built up over a long period of time.

After months of waiting, thankfully, the final ruling only took about five minutes. The relief was indescribable. Finally, our fight was over, and at last we could rejoice in the knowledge that justice had been upheld. Rachel could now rest peacefully.

The outcome of the appeal was a very well-deserved victory for the Gardaí, as each and every one of them who was involved in the case had worked so hard for so long. Our country should be very proud of them. Without their efforts, we probably would not have seen justice.

We were very lucky things turned out as they did and that we were able to see justice being done for Rachel – other families have not been so fortunate. When someone commits such a horrific crime as planning and carrying out the taking of somebody's life and is found guilty before a judge and jury, their sentence should always reflect the awful crime they have committed. This is not how things always turn out in criminal trials. Criminals can be sentenced to life in prison, but life should really mean life. As it is now, 'life in prison' can mean a lot of things, and to me, in my ignorance, it just does not seem fair and in many cases does not reflect the act committed so there is no deterrent against such crimes. My biggest hope is the people who make our laws will get some backbone and realize the state our beautiful country is really in when it comes to the state of our criminal justice system. Our family succeeded in getting justice, but every day the news tells of yet another vile murder, and with each passing day, the violence in our society seems to be getting worse. More and more families are experiencing the hell that it is to lose a loved one through violence, and still the old system is upheld, and the perpetrators are often handled with kid gloves. I would love to see the laws being made to deal with our changing times; the old ways are not working, and the decent people of Ireland would back our politicians who are brave enough to try to tackle this nightmare situation. The will to do so would take bravery and courage, I know, but those people brave enough would receive a great amount of support. We, the ordinary people of Ireland, are tired of it; we have had enough. Having seen what the law can do to help families of victims, we are even more aware of how badly the law could have worked against us, and we have every sympathy with people who are finding it a struggle to get justice for their loved ones.

20. The Aftermath ... and Remembering Rachel

As I sit writing this, almost four and a half years have passed since Rachel was taken from us in such a very cruel way. Life feels so different to all of us now. It is the worst pain imaginable to lose a child, but to learn of their brutal murder at the hands of the person they had most loved and trusted is just something that I cannot come to terms with – I doubt I ever will. I miss her so much. Never again to hear her cheery 'Hi, Mam' as she comes through the front door with the children; never to hear her voice on the phone as she rings to say she is on her way to take me shopping. I miss her infectious love of life. I miss her on her birthday and Mother's Day and all the special days we celebrate as a family. Christmas will never be the same for me. I still love it, and it is a very special family time for us, but with a big difference, Rachel is not here any longer, and only we know how that loss affects us. Life still goes on, but it is changed for ever.

Since the conviction of Rachel's murderer in July 2007 and his subsequent incarceration, you would think that we could get some closure and salvage what we could of our lives. At the beginning of the new year in 2008, as I was closing the front door and I called to Paul to come witness the glorious sunset that lit up the sky so warmly even though it was bitterly cold and snowy and really felt like winter outside, at that moment I could not help but wonder how many sunsets and rainbows had I missed out on in the previous few years. Rachel loved rainbows, and I never look upon a brilliant sunset or rainbow without picturing her there right in the middle of it. There was something that I heard once that has always stayed in my mind: 'May we never miss a sunset or a rainbow because we are looking down.' I realized my head had been down too much, and my new year's resolution was to be conscious of what I was missing.

We had gone through hell for the last three and a half years, and the stress and anguish we have had to endure is beyond belief. Our daughter Ann was very involved in events leading up to this point, and she has paid a great price. Midway through January 2008, Ann thought that she had an eye infection, but very quickly we discovered that it was much more serious than that. We thought the problem was solved, but she continued to have problems and was diagnosed with a tumour behind her eye. The tumour was removed quickly, and thankfully the operation was a great success, but later a biopsy revealed it was not benign, but cancerous. I do not know how she has coped so well so far; she is an example to all of us. She has needed every ounce of her boundless energy to get through the vigorous schedule of operations, chemotherapy and radiotherapy treatments. By the time this book is published, she will be at the end of a long, hard road. We are assured that, at the end of the treatment, she will be completely cured, and the prognosis is great, thank God. We are devastated that Ann should have to endure so much, having already been through so much heartache; it does not seem fair. Sometimes, I just do not know what to say any more. Sometimes, I feel I am hurtling through white rapids in a giant eggshell and heading straight for the falls, so much has befallen our family, but it is simply a matter of getting through each hour as it comes. I keep telling Ann that this time next year, please God, the treatment will all be over, and we will be back to normal again.

Even though I carry with me a fear of the future, I count my blessings once more for the sincere and compassionate help that Ann has received from all the doctors, nurses and medical staff concerned; it has done a great deal to restore our faith in humanity. There is so much goodness out there, and the knowledge that so much help was offered by such skilled, busy people has left us humbled. Please God by the time this book is finished, Ann's journeys through the rapids will have ended, and life will hopefully start being good to her, God knows she deserves it. As Ann says herself, she knows Rachel has been with her every step of the way.

Each day, our memories of Rachel are part of what allows us to try to move forward with our lives in the aftermath of the trauma of the whole ordeal. Each one of us in our family holds dear our time with Rachel, and we are always aware of her presence among us.

After the trial, we went on a family holiday to Lanzarote. Jim, Ann and I visited a tourist centre called Los Jameos del Agua that was created by the famous artist César Manrique. We were sitting in one of the gardens, enjoying its beauty, when

I noticed that Ann had tears falling down her face. As I followed her gaze, I saw a young couple walking slowly by on the far side of the pool. I almost fainted with shock. The girl looked so much like Rachel it was hard to believe. She had the very same build, the same hair colour and style – she even moved and walked exactly like her. We were all very upset as it brought home to us how she should still be with us every day. We have all had many experiences just like this one – we seem to see Rachel in the most unexpected places. It just makes us realize that she is with us even if we can't see her.

The lyrics of particular songs remind us of Rachel and how much she loved music; I had never sat next to her in her car without her having a CD or the radio on. One of her favourites was *The Ultimate Chick Flick Love Songs*. Ann has a copy of the CD Rachel always kept in her car and used to play non-stop. After she died, at first I used to cry all the time when I heard music on the car radio that reminded me of her. I still find travelling on my own in the car very hard. I cannot explain it but I can almost feel her there beside me.

Rachel has been here with me as I have tried to give her a voice throughout this book. I need her and miss her so much and I hope she is happy with what I have written. My one wish is that she will never be forgotten, but if the love and support shown for her to us in the past four and a half years by the people of Ireland is anything to go by, I know she never will be. Indeed, as the months passed after Rachel's trial, there were times I was feeling very, very down when something would arrive in the post from a total stranger, letting us know that we were not forgotten and, indeed, that people were still praying for us. Going through a lengthy trial was very isolating, as we had spent so much time away from our normal lives, our families and our friends. It was hugely comforting to know that we were getting such support from the rest of the country. It would brighten up my whole day when I collected those letters from the porch. They always seemed to arrive at the time when I needed them the most. These letters were such a big part of our healing that I want everyone who wrote to us to know what their support meant to us. Just knowing that so many people cared about Rachel and were praying for justice eased our very heavy burden.

I just wish that everyone who wrote to us could have known her for themselves. It will always be a challenge to keep looking forward and to try to come to terms with the reality of life as it now exists for us, each in our own way. It is only when you experience a dreadful event such as this that you realize how many more families are affected beyond your own, and I wish there was something I could do to make a difference to them as they have for us. Even now, it is wonderful to reread the letters and tributes to Rachel and to know how much she was loved, and I still get great strength from them today.

I will always be so grateful to the whole nation for the way they took Rachel to their hearts. They will never know how much their support sustained us. The following are just a few of the letters we have received over the past few years. I thank those involved for their permission to have them published and I just wish that there was room in this book to publish them all.

Dublin 13
October 2004

Dear Mr & Mrs Callaly,
My deepest sympathy and sadness on the loss of your
beautiful Rachel.
My husband and I had the pleasure of meeting Rachel
some years ago. Every time we met we were struck by her
openness, generosity and kindness. I only spoke to her
recently and as always she was all about the children

and the same fun girl who had won a very special place in our hearts.

I can only say you are all in our thoughts and prayers. Just know Rachel's spirit will always be with those she loves.

If there is anything I can do to help you please do not hesitate to ring me.

Yours sincerely,
Lillian Jones

Dunmore East
July 2007

Dear Rose, Jim and Family
This is just to let you know we are all thinking of you and praying for justice for your family. My heart breaks when I see you all having to face such an ordeal every day. I ask God to give you all strength to get through this terrible time. God bless.

Love & best wishes from Annie [Molloy]

Dublin 24
October 2004

Dear Mr & Mrs Callaly
I just want to say that my memories of Rachel are of a beautiful happy young woman. As a client of Ian Kenny

Boyd I had a lot of dealings with Rachel. At all times
she made you feel so important. We often had little chats
on diets, the gym etc. and not forgetting her little children.
She is a great loss, not just to her family but to everyone
who was privileged to know her. May she rest in
peace.
  Yours sincerely
  Margaret Kenny

Co Dublin
October 2005

To Mr & Mrs Callaly & Family,
I meant to put pen to paper before now but kept living
in the hope that Rachel's killer would be brought to justice.
I live 'around the corner' at the Nag's Head and was
one of the many friends Rachel made when she moved to
Naul. I used to walk past her house nearly every day
and she always had a big wave and a big smile. She
extended the hand of friendship to me in a way that no
one else ever had. She introduced me to Helen and the
play school and we had planned to share 'the school
run'.
  I will never forget her vibrance and energy. She inspired
me with her love for life. I pray for her every day and
also pray that justice will be done.
  My sincere sympathy goes out to you all, especially at the

time of her anniversary, may God give you all strength to
continue the fight.
   Yours sincerely,
   Louise McEvoy

This letter was addressed to Rachel's children, to be
given to them when they are older.

Co Dublin
4 October 2005

This time last year the community was in shock at the
terrible loss of a great member, a neighbour and a friend –
yes, your wonderful mum Rachel! A year has gone by and
we all miss her so much and think about her every day. We
also think of you two and feel so sad for the times you will
miss with Rachel and all the hopes, dreams and plans she
had for both of you. No child should be deprived of their
mother and no mothers be deprived of seeing their children
grow up.
   I met your mum for the first time in September 2004.
I know she was a very good friend of my sister [Fidelma
Geraghty] and knew from my sister that Rachel was a
lovely person. Then one day while preparing for a protest
campaign against a super-dump in our community, Sarah
Harmon introduced me to Rachel. I was sitting in the
kitchen of Sarah's house when in arrived Rachel with a

*big smile on her face and shook hands warmly with me.
I will always remember the way she filled that room with
her presence as she walked in, asking 'where are you?'
I realized she was looking for her two beautiful children,
who were walking in behind her.*

*From that moment I felt as if I had known Rachel all
my life as she had that wonderful unique way about her.
I am only sorry I didn't know her longer! Rachel called to
my home after that and I began to realize that this lovely
person was a very giving person and wanted to help with
the campaign more and more.*

*She and I got talking about my husband John being an
ex-international cyclist and she realized that her dad Jim
must have known John. When she asked John it turned out
that your granddad Callaly knew John and your cousin
Jim Callaly [Rachel's first cousin, also a cyclist] is a good
friend of ours. Rachel was delighted to make the connection
and we joked about it many times.*

*I can't remember ever seeing your mum over the weeks I
was lucky enough to know her without both of you by her
side. One always in school uniform and the other in a buggy
as your mum rushed around helping and attending our
protest marches. It was during one of these protests where
I brought a small school blackboard and wrote on it 'Don't
Poison Our School' and gave it to you to hold. Rachel loved
the idea and asked me if you could keep it so that she could
take your photo at home with it. I am not sure if she ever*

got the chance to take that photo but I know she was so proud of you both being on the march with her. Wanting to take that photo showed me once again that no matter what she was involved in her two beautiful children were part of it. You were her life then and every day of your lives is living proof that Rachel was here and is here. You are both her flesh and blood and I have no doubt her loving and caring ways will shine through you both all your lives. One thing you can be certain of – you both have a loving guardian angel looking over you always.

Rachel will never be gone from our hearts and memories. May she rest in peace and may you both get some kind of comfort knowing that she loved you both so much and that you both look so much like her which is living proof Rachel Callaly lived and loved!
Marian Shortt Nevitt

Dublin 9
July 2007

Dear Rose, Jim & Family
I knew Rachel through our mutual best friend Jackie. She was a beautiful person, thoughtful and funny and just like you describe – a ray of sunshine with always a beaming smile. She was a fantastic mum to her children, living for them (often declining a girls' night out because she was a mum). My thoughts and prayers are constantly with her,

the children and your family and I hope and pray for peace
and reconciliation.

Rachel Fox & family

Dublin 9
July 2007

To Rose, Jim, Ann and children
You've been in our constant thoughts and prayers these
past 2½ years but particularly these past three weeks.
Glad you are all relieved and may peace be restored to your
lives again. You will continue to be remembered in our
prayers.

Anne & Jerry, Bryan and all the Costelloes

Dublin 9
July 2007

Dear Mr & Mrs Callaly
I'll always remember the day I heard the news on the
radio that a mother was killed in her home in The Naul.
I felt so sorry for her and her family. Like many others I
followed the story in the papers and I could not believe
it.

I am so sorry for your loss. I can't imagine the pain you
have felt and still feel. My family and I pray for you and
your family, especially Rachel's two children. And we wish

you strength to cope and warm wishes. And finally a 'well done' for the last few weeks.

Yours faithfully
Emer McCrudden & family

Dundalk
August 2007

Dear Rose, Jim and family
My name is Mary and from seeing Rachel and yourselves on TV and newspapers over the last few years, my heart has just gone out to you. I've been wanting to write for a long time. I just wanted to send you this little card and let you know that Rachel and yourselves have been in my thoughts and prayers and still are. You are such a lovely family and no one should ever have to go through what you have been through. Rachel was so beautiful from seeing the many photos of her in the paper, video clips on TV etc. and also such a lovely person from what I've read. I always prayed right from the start that justice would be done and thank God it has. I was so relieved that Saturday evening when I heard the verdict. I know none of this can bring Rachel back for you or take away the terrible pain, but at least he has not got away with it and is not walking free. I hope I haven't upset you by writing. I just felt so sad for you all. Anyway, I will end here. Rachel and yourselves will be in my prayers.

Take care
God bless you
Not forgetting the two little children, hoping that you will
be able to see them as much as you want to.
Mary Bell

Cork
July 2007

Dear Mr & Mrs Callaly & Family
Sorry for taking so long in writing to you, as it's so hard
to put on paper how we feel. I know justice has been done,
thank God, and I hope justice will continue for Rachel,
for her two little children and for you all.
Rachel, in silence you suffered and the nation grieved
for you.
Irene O'Sullivan and all the O'Sullivan Family

Killarney
July 2007

Dear Rose and family
Both you and your family have been an inspiration to
everyone in Ireland. Your dignity and composure, and most
of all your faith, was so evident in all the turmoil. Your
family are a credit to you both. Everyone could see the

beautiful girl you've lost but because of you she will never be forgotten.

Seanie & Eileen Kelliher

Dublin 14
July 2007

Dear Rose, Jim and family
All our thoughts and prayers have been with you over the last difficult time. We have all grown to know your beautiful Rachel and her family and will always remember her in our prayers. You are such a wonderful person and you have had me in tears, talking with motherly love. I wish you and Jim peace in your life now and may Rachel rest in peace. You are such an inspiration. God bless, always.

Anne Egan

Co Wexford
July 2007

Dear Rose & Jim
Just a note to say how delighted we are to hear of the outcome. My heart went out to you all for the last three years, and especially in the last few very hard weeks you all had to go through.

Having only lately become a mother myself, and aged 30

this year, I could not think of being taken from my child. It seems so unfair that your beautiful daughter, Rachel, was. I just felt I need to send you a note, and I am sure Rachel is very proud of her family and will rest in peace. Please keep strong as a family and look after yourselves now, and try to get plenty of rest.

I think you have touched the whole of Ireland and be very proud of the way you were all so together, composed and united as a family.

Yours faithfully
Joe, Carol & baby Charlie (Ellard) xxxx

Dublin 7
July 2007

To the Callaly Family
I have had a Mass said for you. I hope it will help in some small way to ease your suffering. You are a remarkable family. You have shown such strength and dignity at a time of unbelievable tragedy. May the Lord shower His Blessings on you. May Rachel rest in peace.

Yours sincerely
Kathleen Nugent & family

Co Wexford
July 2007

Dear Rose, Jim and family
This is one of the happiest letters I have ever written: justice
has now been served! The whole of Ireland was with you.
And any appeal will have to be based on a point of law,
which would have to find Judge Barry White in error in his
conduct of the trial. He was a very very fair judge.

As for the Callaly family! Rachel will be so very proud of
you all. She could never have asked for a stronger more
loving Mam, Dad, brothers and sister. Take time out now
(if possible) to relax and feel her hugging each and every
one of you.

My thoughts are with you all
With love
Liz Donnelly & family

Co Kilkenny
July 2007

Dear Mr and Mrs Callaly
Please excuse this intrusion but upon reading about your
beloved daughter Rachel in the paper today I came upon
your address.

I am just writing to say how very sorry I am for the loss
of your beautiful daughter. To lose a child does not bear

thinking about and having two wonderful daughters myself (one a Rachel also!) I cannot begin to imagine the grief and pain both of you and your family are living with. In particular the callous manner in which your Rachel was taken from this life is unimaginable.

You are both fantastic brave and loving parents. Your daughter Rachel was an absolutely beautiful person both in appearance and by all accounts in person. She too was a fantastic mother to her two children. The strength and composure evident by you both over the last number of weeks were simply astounding and I have no doubt that Rachel was looking down from heaven with great pride.

Having just watched your interview on RTÉ this evening I was so impressed by your composure and strength of character. As you said, Mrs Callaly, 'If you put out good it comes back to you . . .' How very true. I only hope and pray that I am half as good a parent to my two young daughters as you both obviously are. Thank God justice prevailed in this case.

Once again, apologies for this intrusion but just to say how wonderful you both are, and your family. I was so upset and enraged on hearing some of the evidence over the past number of weeks and I thought how upsetting and harrowing it must have been for all of you to have to listen to that said about Rachel. You are all in my

thoughts and prayers and in particular Rachel's two lovely
children.

    Yours sincerely
    Nicola Dwyer

Co Mayo
July 2007

Dear Mr & Mrs Callaly & family
As a member of the general public I would like to convey
my sympathy to you on the tragic loss of your beautiful
daughter Rachel. Like everyone in Ireland I was horrified
by what had happened to her. I would like to commend you
on your bravery in the most difficult of times and also for
the love and loyalty you have shown in public for Rachel.
You have done her proud by speaking so eloquently about
her and as a result she will always be remembered as the
beautiful girl that she was.

    May I wish you all the very best as you try to get your
lives together and hope you know that I and others will
be thinking of you and offering up a prayer for you in the
days ahead.

    Yours sincerely
    Mary McDonnell

Dublin 9
December 2008

Dear Mr & Mrs Callaly
You don't know me. I hope you don't mind me writing to
you. I simply want to say that my thoughts and prayers are
with you and your family this Christmas season. I have
daughters around Rachel's age and hardly a day passes
when I don't think of you. I hope you experience some of
the peace and joy of Christmas time.
  God bless all your family
  Yours very sincerely
  Hilda Smith

Dublin 5
June 2007

Dear Rose,
I feel I must write to you to let you know that my thoughts
and prayers are with you and Jim and family during
these very sad days. I can not imagine how difficult it is for
you all, as you relive the terrible tragedy of the cruel death
of your beloved Rachel. You were very brave yesterday —
outwardly so calm and dignified but inwardly so heart-
broken. God gave you the strength and courage to face this
awful ordeal — I pray that He will be by your side always.
I think of your dear mother during these days and am glad

that she is spared this terrible pain. Her heart broke when she heard of Rachel's death – almost three years ago. Now they are both with God and at peace. I am praying to your good mother for you Rose, that she will help you from Heaven. May God comfort you all and support you with His love. With every good wish and many prayers for all,

Yours sincerely,

Breege McCarrick

Dublin 5

September 2007

Dear Rose and Family,

I can never thank you enough for your beautiful letter and Rachel's memoriam card. I will treasure them forever. I cried my eyes out when I opened the envelope. You are such an amazing person to take the time to do that with all you have been through. You are an amazing family and carry yourselves with such dignity and grace. It's thanks to you that people like me got to know Rachel as the wonderful person she was and not another name in the paper. You allowed the country know what a kind, loving mother, sister, friend and daughter she was. I know she is so proud of you all and will always be with you.

Yours faithfully,

Karen Perkins and family

As I reach the end of this book, I am hoping that we, as a family, will get back to some level of normality, please God. Life can never be the same again, as the whole experience has taken a big toll on all of our family, but I hope with all my heart that we can get on with our lives.

When I started to write, I would have to leave it for weeks at a time as I would become so upset and angry. The anger I felt was not what I wanted, as I knew how destructive it could be. I hoped that it would get easier as Rachel's story unfolded, and as I wrote out everything that happened, but it was not to be. At one stage, I even decided to abandon my plan of writing Rachel's story, because it was just so distressing to write down every thought that I had been trying to suppress in my attempts to maintain a normal life. In the end, I managed it, but only just. I would write during the day and spend my nights wide awake with everything I had written turning over and over in my mind. The process seemed to bury me, as I felt like I was passing my days and nights in a big black hole with no way out. I know I got there thanks to Rachel's help. She is the brightest star I see when I look up at the night sky, the comforting presence that walks with me along the cliff paths, forest walks or by the shore. She never leaves my mind and is my constant companion, but I wish I could be given another chance to have her back again. It is the reality of knowing that can never happen that is so very hard to live with.

I always feel very sad when I see apples growing on those trees that Rachel planted and know that she is no longer around to see them. Parts of her spirit have been left in the most unexpected places, and, whatever eventually happens to that house in Baldarragh, Rachel's presence will live in everybody's memory. I only have to think of her and she might as well be right here beside me. Her beautiful spirit will always stay with me, and I know that some day I will be able to make sense of it all. I hope the sun is shining on her all the time now, and that she feels very much loved and cherished. I know that, wherever she is, it is a better place since she has arrived there.

Acknowledgements

There are so many people who have my deepest gratitude for all their support, friendship, prayers and love, so many in fact that it would be impossible to name each one. I want them all to know that, just because I do not mention them here by name, it does not mean I have forgotten the part they played in getting us through the past five years of surviving this horror. Sitting writing this book took me once again through all of my worst nightmares. Having to relive memories that are so awful, at times, I truly felt I was losing my sanity; however, with Rachel by my side and the love and support I received, it has finally come to fruition.

First, I would like to thank my daughter Ann for her love, patience and help in making this book a reality – without her constant encouragement and hard work, it could not have happened. Also to my husband Jim and my three sons, Declan, Paul and Anthony, who stayed with me through the ups and downs and persuaded me to keep at it by showing their faith and belief in me. Thanks also to my two daughters-in-law, Denise and Denise, who have always been so supportive, and to our six beautiful grandchildren, Rachel's two little ones, and Lauren, Sam, Dakota and Skye, who light up our lives. I will always be thankful for their love, encouragement and support.

Heartfelt thanks to my sister Susan and her husband Kevin and to the rest of my siblings, Charlie, Jimmy, Tony, Christy, Ray, Eugene and Sindy, and all their families, and to each of Jim's brothers, Kevin, Tom and John, and their families – I wish to thank them for their love and support in getting us through the bad times.

A special word of thanks to Paul Reynolds for his advice and guidance. A debt of gratitude to my agent, Faith O'Grady, and all at Penguin Ireland and UK, specifically Patricia Deevy, Michael McLoughlin, Patricia McVeigh, Cliona Lewis and Brian Walker. I would also like to thank editors Nora Mahony and David Watson, who were instrumental in the production of this book.

I would like to pay tribute to the Gardaí in Balbriggan and the National Bureau of Criminal Investigation in Harcourt Square, as I truly feel that, but for all their dedication and hard work, Rachel's killer would not have been convicted and this book would not have come into existence. In particular our heartfelt thanks to the men we got to know over the years and who will never be forgotten by us. First, Superintendent Tom Gallagher, who retired from the Gardaí before the trial and was succeeded by Superintendent Joe Kelly, whom we would also like to thank most sincerely. Despite having retired, Superintendent Gallagher made it his business to be there at the trial and was a reassuring presence for us. Next were Detectives Pat Marry and Peter McCoy, who were the most familiar to us and were such a great support to our family in helping us through the whole ordeal. Special thanks to Detective Garda Sean Fitzpatrick, Detective Garda Jim McGovern, Detective Garda John Clancy and Detective Sergeant John Geraghty for their excellent work and consistent support at the courts.

Since the trial, Detective Sergeant Pat Marry has been promoted to Inspector and is now stationed at Drogheda Garda Station. Detective Peter McCoy has retired from the Garda Síochána after a long and loyal service. We wish each and every one involved in the case the very best of luck in their future. I know Rachel would have been very proud of all that was done on her behalf.

A special word of heartfelt gratitude to Oliver Farrell, Karim Benabdullah and Enda Furlong, who by their expert testimony successfully demonstrated in a very simple way the workings of the mobile phone network, making it possible for the inexperienced general public to understand the technological evidence. I would like them to know how grateful our family will always be to them.

I just do not have the words to explain what the support, care and love we received from the public meant to us. We knew we were not alone; they took Rachel to their hearts and have never forgotten her since. We will always be very grateful to all who worked on the case from the DPP's office and the prosecution team: we will never forget your diligence and expertise.

A special word of thanks to Agnes for her encouragement and generosity, and to all of our friends who have supported us in whatever way they could. We are so grateful and lucky to be blessed with such great friendship, love and support from all.

He just wanted a decent book to read ...

Not too much to ask, is it? It was in 1935 when Allen Lane, Managing Director of Bodley Head Publishers, stood on a platform at Exeter railway station looking for something good to read on his journey back to London. His choice was limited to popular magazines and poor-quality paperbacks – the same choice faced every day by the vast majority of readers, few of whom could afford hardbacks. Lane's disappointment and subsequent anger at the range of books generally available led him to found a company – and change the world.

'We believed in the existence in this country of a vast reading public for intelligent books at a low price, and staked everything on it'
Sir Allen Lane, 1902–1970, founder of Penguin Books

The quality paperback had arrived – and not just in bookshops. Lane was adamant that his Penguins should appear in chain stores and tobacconists, and should cost no more than a packet of cigarettes.

Reading habits (and cigarette prices) have changed since 1935, but Penguin still believes in publishing the best books for everybody to enjoy. We still believe that good design costs no more than bad design, and we still believe that quality books published passionately and responsibly make the world a better place.

So wherever you see the little bird – whether it's on a piece of prize-winning literary fiction or a celebrity autobiography, political tour de force or historical masterpiece, a serial-killer thriller, reference book, world classic or a piece of pure escapism – you can bet that it represents the very best that the genre has to offer.

Whatever you like to read – trust Penguin.